# Preaching Through the Bible

## Judges and Ruth

## Michael Eaton

## Sovereign World

Sovereign World
PO Box 777
Tonbridge
Kent, TN11 0ZS
England

*By the same author:*
*Genesis 1–11* (Preaching Through the Bible) – Sovereign World
*Genesis 12–23* (Preaching Through the Bible) – Sovereign World
*Genesis 24–50* (Preaching Through the Bible) – Sovereign World
*Applying God's Law* (Exodus 19–24) – Paternoster
*Joshua* (Preaching Through the Bible) – Sovereign World
*1 Samuel* (Preaching Through the Bible) – Sovereign World
*2 Samuel* (Preaching Through the Bible) – Sovereign World
*1 Kings* (Preaching Through the Bible) – Sovereign World
*Ecclesiastes* (Tyndale Commentary) – IVP
*Hosea* (Focus on the Bible) – Christian Focus
*Joel and Amos* (Preaching Through the Bible) – Sovereign World
*The Way That Leads to Life* (Matthew 5–7) – Christian Focus
*Mark* (Preaching Through the Bible) – Sovereign World
*Return to Glory* (Romans 3:22–5:21) – Paternoster
*Living Under Grace* (Romans 6–7) – Paternoster
*1 Corinthians 1–9* (Preaching Through the Bible) – Sovereign World
*1, 2 Thessalonians* (Preaching Through the Bible) – Sovereign World
*2 Timothy* (Preaching Through the Bible) – Sovereign World
*1 Peter* (Preaching Through the Bible) – Sovereign World
*1, 2, 3 John* (Focus on the Bible) – Christian Focus
*Living A Godly Life* (Theology for Beginners) – Paternoster
*Enjoying God's Worldwide Church* (Theology for Beginners) – Paternoster
*No Condemnation* – IVCP (USA)
*Experiencing God* (Theology for Beginners) – Paternoster

ISBN: 1-85240-291-1

Typeset by CRB Associates, Reepham, Norfolk
Printed in England by Clays Ltd, St Ives plc.

# General Preface

There is need of a series of biblical expositions which are especially appropriate for English-speaking people throughout the world. Such expositions need to be laid out in such a way that they will be useful to those who like to have their material or (if they are preachers) to put across their material in clear points. They need to avoid difficult vocabulary and advanced grammatical structures. They need to avoid European or North American illustrations. *Preaching Through the Bible* seeks to meet such a need. Although intended for an international audience I have no doubt that their simplicity of language will be of interest to many first-language speakers of English as well.

These expositions are based upon the Hebrew and Greek texts. The New American Standard Version and the New International Version of the Bible are recommended to the reader, but at times the expositor will simply translate the Hebrew or Greek himself.

It is not our purpose to deal with minute exegetical detail, although the commentator has to do work of this nature as part of his preliminary preparation. But just as a housewife likes to serve a good meal rather than display her pots and pans, so we are concerned with the 'good meal' of Scripture, rather than the 'pots and pans' of dictionaries, disputed interpretations and the like. Only occasionally will such matters have to be discussed. Similarly matters of 'Introduction' do not receive detailed discussion, but only as much as is necessary for the exposition to be clear. On occasions a simple outline of some 'introductory' matters will be included, perhaps in an appendix, but the first chapter of each exposition gets into the message of Scripture as speedily as possible.

Although on the surface written simply, these expositions aim at a high level of scholarship, and attempt to put the theological and practical message of each book of the Bible in a clear and down-to-earth manner. Simplicity of style is not simplicity of content. God's word should be expounded with thoroughness, but the language needs to remain easy and accessible. Some progress in this direction is attempted in these expositions.

*Michael A. Eaton*

# Contents

# Author's Preface

These studies on Judges and Ruth arise out of my work of
preaching through Scripture. I have twice preached through
the book of Ruth, in Johannesburg and in Nairobi. The Book
of Judges was the basis of much of my preaching during
July–August 1997, in Mumbai, India, and in various cities of
South Africa. To the many fellowships in which I ministered
during those months, I am most grateful. For their hospitality, warmth and Christian fellowship, I am grateful to David
Fernandes, Arun Philip, and to Colin and Nawaz D'Cruz who
were my hosts at that time.

My travels in South Africa and Zambia later on in 1997
gave me further opportunities to speak on different aspects of
the message of Judges. Some of these chapters were written in
the Johannesburg home of Jochen and Violet Stutzner who
have for many years been faithful and hospitable friends to
me and my family.

As always I am grateful for the support of family and
friends who encourage my preaching and writing. My spiritual home in the Chrisco churches of Nairobi is precious
to me indeed. Friends in Nairobi City Hall lunchtime
meetings, in the Discipleship School, in Central Church, in
KICC Chrisco Church, and other Chrisco venues, heard
some of these chapters after I got back from my travels in
India, South Africa and Zambia. They are precious friends
indeed.

To Jenny; to Tina Gysling, my daughter, who works through my material; to my son Calvin who is an ever-present help to me; to Chris Mungeam, a faithful friend – many thanks.

*Michael A. Eaton*

# *Chapter 1*

# The 'Third Generation'

(Judges 1:1–21)

The Book of Judges tells what happened from the third generation onwards, after Israel's deliverance from bondage in Egypt. The great act of God in which He saved Israel by the blood of a lamb took place probably between 1290 and 1260 BC (let us say 1275 BC). The Book of Judges deals with a period of Israel's history that runs from about 1195 to 1050 BC.

Imagine a great event in the story of a nation. It might be a great victory after a time of war; it might be a day of independence or freedom. The generation that went through those events are constantly gripped with the memory of what happened. The next generation grows up with parents who are constantly talking of 'the war' or 'the day we got our freedom' – or whatever. Then there grows up a third generation. By the time they are born, the events of two generations before are dim. Their parents sometimes talk about what **their** parents used to talk about, but the events are no longer in **living** memory and do not arouse the excitement that they aroused in their grandparents.

Something like this happened in Israel. God had saved Israel by the blood of a lamb. Pharaoh had been punished by ten mighty judgements. The Sea of Reeds had been dramatically divided and the people had walked across dry land before the sea came flooding back again. The generation who experienced those events could never completely forget what had happened.

Then there was the persistent disobedience of Israel while they were in the wilderness between Egypt and Canaan. Eventually God left that generation in the wilderness for forty years. The time came when all the adults who had experienced the crossing of the Sea of Reeds had died. Only a few who had been children or teenagers at the time were alive to remember what had happened.

Then during another forty-year generation Joshua and his soldiers conquered the main highways of Israel and devastated the greatest of the Canaanite cities. At the time when Joshua died it was eighty years after Israel's salvation through the blood of the lamb. There was no one alive who remembered exactly what that day had been like in experience. Judges tells of what happened next. In Judges 1:1–3:6 (which itself divides into two, 1:1–2:5; 2:6–3:6) we are told of the decline of Israel.

In Judges 3:7–16:31 we have the story of twelve judges plus the story of Abimelech's experiment with kingship.

In Judges 17:1–21:25 we have (again in two units, 17:1–18:31; 19:1–21:25) a description of the chaos in Israel at the end of this period.

There are two main things we ought to note at this point.

1. **For a while Israel continued to live for God but its victories were only partial**. These people were 'third generation believers'. They were people for whom salvation was not as real as it had been for believers of an earlier time. Israel had partially but not entirely conquered the promised land.

Judah was the tribe most notable for its victories (Judges 1:1–20). There are four ingredients in its partial success.

**Judah's victory came by seeking God**. The people inquire which tribe shall attack Canaan first (1:1) and they get the answer: Judah (1:2). Presumably they consulted the 'Urim and Thummim', the stones kept in the high priests coat that could be thrown like dice. The way they landed could reveal the will of God. They could say 'yes', 'no' or give no answer. The Lord guided them to send Judah first to attack the 'Canaanites' (which here means the inhabitants of the valleys and coastal plains). Victory comes by God's guidance!

**Judah's victory came by co-operation**. Judah asked for the help of their brother-tribe, the tribe of Simeon (1:3); together they got victory (1:4).

**Judah's victory led to justice being executed**. Azoni-bezek, a pagan king, is captured (1:5) and mutilated (1:6). He dies confessing the justice of his punishment (1:7). He was receiving the treatment he had given out to others.

**Judah's victory is the attaining of inheritance**. Jerusalem is attacked (1:8) and so are the three major geographical divisions of southern Israel (1:9). Caleb led an attack on Hebron and three other towns (1:10–11). Othniel won Caleb's daughter in marriage by capturing Kiriath-sepher (1:12–13). His newly acquired bride asked for water-springs to be added to her inheritance (1:14–15). Inheritance is one of the great themes of the Bible. The Christian is saved in order to 'inherit'. Israel was rescued from Egypt in order to 'inherit'.

Allied to Judah were the Kenites, a people friendly to Israel who became part of the nation. The narrator tells us of the area inhabited by them (1:16). Judah assisted Simeon in conquering Zephath (1:17), and he took Gaza and Ashkelon and Ekron (1:18), three Philistine cities. All these are examples of God's people 'inheriting' as a result of persistent God-guided conflict against the enemies of God. The Christian also has his 'inheritance'. It includes areas of life which God gives us to 'conquer' for him. It consists of the joy of entering into rest in that realm which God gives us to 'conquer' for him.

2. **There was one great failure in this 'third generation': they failed to follow through with what God was calling them to do**. They conquered Jerusalem (1:8) but obviously neglected to totally occupy it (as the later story makes clear). It is clear that Israel's victories were limited. The Kenites lived **among** the Amorite people of the wilderness of Judea (1:16). Although some cities were destroyed (see 1:17–18), yet Judges 1:19 tells us some people could not be driven out of the plains. Although Caleb drove out three sons of Anak (1:20), yet the Jebusites could not be totally dislodged from Jerusalem (1:21).

The best generation in Israel's history was the second generation, the people who followed God in the wilderness (see Jeremiah 2:2–3, and the rebuke of Jeremiah 2:4–13). The people of Judges 1:1–3:6 were a more complacent people, lacking the faith of the previous generation.

'Third generation' believers fail to carry forward the work of God to an advanced state of victory. They carry things forward a little but are more or less content with what they had been left by their parents.

'Third generation' believers get used to the 'status quo' – the state things have been in within the memory of their times. They think of the great events of days gone by as just that – events of days gone by. They do not imagine that God can do something as wonderful in their day as God did for others in previous days. In reality God can do something different but equally great!

Every Christian needs to be in touch with God for himself. His parents may well have been truly saved. Yet the son or daughter needs to experience God for themselves, and follow God fully, not living on previous achievements but building on them and achieving for God more than was done before.

# Chapter 2

## Being Given What You Want

### (Judges 1:22–2:5)

Luz, later known as Bethel, was destroyed with the help of a man who betrayed the city in the same way that Rahab betrayed Jericho (1:22–26). But unlike Rahab he seems to have had no faith in the God of Israel. He did not join Israel but went elsewhere and built a new Luz. Rahab acted from faith; this man acted from compulsion and no more.

The Canaanites were not totally driven out by Israel. The tribe of Manasseh failed to conquer the territory offered to it (1:27–28) and allowed Canaanites to live Manasseh's territory. The same policy was followed by Ephraim (1:29), Zebulon (1:30), Asher (1:31–32), Naphtali (1:33).

The case of the Danites was even worse. For a while the people of the tribe of Dan were prevented from occupying their lowland territory (1:34–35a); later the 'Joseph-tribes' grew in power (1:35b) and the Amorites (another name for Canaanites) were confined to the areas mentioned in 1:36.

There are several aspects to Israel's backsliding ways.

1. **It is a serious matter to fail to follow through with what God has ordered**. They **could** have utterly exterminated the Canaanites. They were commanded to do so. It was a unique case in the story of the world. Israel were to be God's executioners. They had been commanded to annihilate the Canaanites altogether. But they failed to do so.

God brought them out of Egypt. There was a possibility of success for them. God said 'I brought you up...' (2:1). Israel's being brought into Canaan was the result of the mighty working of God. He had brought them out of Egypt, and had brought them into Canaan. He told them of His intention that the Canaanites should be destroyed (2:2). But Israel disobeyed the Lord in that they failed to follow through with what God had done for them.

The Israelites were saved by the blood of the lamb but then they were to achieve the conquest of Canaan. The first generation were redeemed by the blood of the lamb. The second generation conquered the main highways and fortresses of Canaan. The third generation should have completed the work and 'entered into rest'. 'Entering into rest' means to reap the great blessing of achieving God's will for one's life. It comes at the point where, after persistent faith, God says 'Now I know that you fear me; I have sworn; I will bless you' (see Genesis 22:12, 16, 17). It does not mean to experience salvation; it does not mean to get to heaven. It means to reap the blessings that come through achieving God's will by faith and patience. But the third generation failed to enter rest; there was a failure to follow through with what God had ordered. David was to finish the task centuries later (see 2 Samuel 7:1).

2. **Sin gets punished by the sin itself**. When God's people sin, it is because they do not think the sin will make much difference to them. But they eventually will get to see that the sin has damaged them, weakened them, and prevented them from achieving as much for God as they could have done.

God said to Israel, in effect, 'Since you don't want to get rid of the Canaanites I will let you keep them nearby!' God lets His people have what they want. He gives them the desires of their hearts – but sometimes this is a punishment. If God's people are half-hearted about getting rid of their spiritual enemies, God leaves them with their enemies! If they do not want to exercise faith, and if they do not persist in the struggle to get rid of the enemies to salvation, then God will leave those enemies where they are – but this will only cause trouble for the people of God. The sin of half-heartedness will bring its own punishment. *'They shall be adversaries to you'*[1] says God (2:3).

Failure to drive out false religion, failure to drive out the remaining sins in our lives – perhaps arrogance, boastfulness, deceit, envy, gossip, impatience, jealousy, negativism, obstinacy, prayerlessness, quarrelsomeness, resentment, spite, talebearing, unbelief, vindictiveness, or whatever – will result in God's chastening by letting that very sin bring distress upon us. *'Their gods shall be a snare to you'* said God. They tolerated the filthy paganism of the Canaanites; soon they would be tempted into the very sins of the Canaanites. If they did not conquer the enemy, the enemy would conquer them. They would become **accustomed** to the sinful ways of their neighbours and then become **attracted** to the sinful ways of their neighbours.

3. **They accepted God's rebuke but their repentance came too late to change the situation**. The 'angel of the Lord' – an angel representing God Himself – appeared at Gilgal. Gilgal was the place where the angel had appeared once before to Joshua to give Joshua assurance that Canaan could be conquered (see Joshua 5:13–15). Now the angel moves through the land to Bochim (near Bethel, or perhaps the same as Bethel) – presumably because the tabernacle was now at Bethel. God announces His verdict: the Canaanites will be left to harass Israel. It is a 'day of visitation'. For a generation God has called them to remove the Canaanites. But they would not. From now on they will no longer be able to do so. When God's people tolerate a situation that is not God's will, eventually they are rebuked by God by their not being able to change the situation. Their sin is forgiven – but the situation remains as a permanent rebuke. The first generation of Israelites were forgiven for their rebelliousness in not entering Canaan (Numbers 14:20) but God's rebuke continued. They **could** not do what at first they **would** not do (see Numbers 14:39–45). The point in Judges 2:4–5 is not that repentance is ineffective or that tears may be insincere; the point is that repentance might bring forgiveness but come too late to avert God's discipline.

# Note

[1] I follow the reading *sarim*, 'adversaries', rather than the Massoretic *siddim*, 'sides', which does not seem to make sense. See Numbers 33:55; Joshua 23:13.

# Chapter 3

## Decline and Renewal
### (Judges 2:6–3:4)

The people of Israel lived together in one camp until Joshua had led them in the conquering of the main centres of Canaan. Then Joshua released the people and allowed them to move to the areas allocated to them (2:6). During the forty years of Joshua's lifetime they remained faithful to Yahweh, the God of Israel (2:7). Then Joshua died (2:8–9) and a new generation grew up *'who did not know Yahweh and did not know what He had done for Israel'* (2:10).

1. **The people of God have within themselves a tendency to decline**. The best thing older believing people can do is encourage a younger generation to discover God for themselves. An up-coming generation has to be able to say to their parents what the people of Samaria said to the Samaritan woman: 'We no longer believe just because of what you said; now we have heard for ourselves...' (John 4:42). If this does not happen, then the passing of the generations produce a spiritual decline in the people of God.

The people of God tend to lapse into **spiritual ignorance**. They 'did not know Yahweh and did not know what He had done...' (2:10).

They adopt **pagan ways** (2:11–12). For the first time since the crossing of Jordan we read of Israel's turning to 'the Baals', the fertility gods and goddesses of ancient paganism. People who lose sight of God tend to turn to what the average pagans around them believe. They adopt their views from majority opinion.

**They lose sight of redemption**. *'They forsook Yahweh ... who had brought them out of Egypt'* (2:12). The fertility gods had not brought Israel newness of life or forgiveness of sins. The Baals had never redeemed them from their enemies in Egypt by the blood of a lamb. Only Yahweh had done that for them. But they forgot their redemption by the blood of a lamb.

**They come under God's anger**. *'They provoked Yahweh...'* says Judges 2:12.

They begin to experience **defeat**. In days gone by they had experienced amazing victories. Think of the things that had happened when they conquered Jericho. But now those experiences of the amazing help of God fell aside and they experienced defeat instead. They forsook Yahweh (2:12). They started worshipping Baal (the god of fertility) and Ashtoreth (the goddess associated with Baal). In His anger God allowed Israel's enemies to dominate the land and trouble the people of Israel. Their crops would be plundered; the people would fall into poverty and slavery at the hands of their enemies (2:14).

They experience **God's opposition** as God had warned them. God swore to give Canaan to Israel (although He did not swear to give it to any particular generation). And He swore He would chastise His people when they sinned. An oath is a promise than cannot be changed. The warnings of Leviticus 26 and Deuteronomy 28 are oaths in the sense that they cannot be changed (but Judges 2:15 is not referring to an oath to a particular generation). 'If you will not obey Yahweh ... Yahweh will cause you to be defeated' (Deuteronomy 28:15, 25). The threat could not be changed. Sin would bring God's opposition and enmity.

2. **Despite their sin, God preserves His people**. What does God do when His people failed to follow through with His instructions? I will tell you what He does **not** do! He does not abandon His people. The gates of death do not prevail against God's plans for the church. Neither Israel nor the church – God's restructured 'Israel' – will ever be wiped off of the face of the earth.

God sent 'saviours' or 'judges'. They were not people who preside in a law-court, but people who execute the decisions and judgements of God. God preserves His people. It would be a long time before God would send David to Israel, and it would be an even longer time before God sent Jesus. Meanwhile God preserved His people by periodically sending to them rescuers and deliverers who brought at least a measure of restoration – until God would act more decisively in David and more decisively still in Jesus.

Yet the 'judges' were only God's temporary measure. In Israel's story the pattern of periodic decline persisted despite occasional times of liberation when God would raise up saviours for His people. *'Then Yahweh raised up judges . . .'* (2:16). These judges were only partially and temporarily successful. They did not totally and permanently restore Israel, because after a while Israel would turn from the ways that the judges had brought in (2:17). They would obey the judge for a while and follow his leadership when he urged them to turn to God (2:18). But once the judge had died they would return to their sinful ways again (2:19).

3. **God tests our allegiance to Him!** God punished Israel by leaving the pagan nations in the land of Canaan (2:20–21). From that point on the pagans were always present. They were a permanent test of obedience for Israel (2:22). At times of disobedience, Israel would adopt their ways. In times of obedience, Israel refused their ways. God allowed those nations to remain in the land (2:23). Although they 'tested' Israel – revealing whether Israel would turn to pagan ways – yet at the same time they were allowed to continue in Israel in order to give the Israelites after the days of Joshua a necessary training in warfare (3:1–2). It was an essential skill while God's people were a nation amidst other nations. Judges 3:3 lists the nations that were involved in this testing and training programme for Israel. The section ends with a key point of the book (the section is best taken as ending at 3:4 rather than 3:6 as is often thought). These nations were left by God to reveal whether or not Israel would obey God.

God preserved His people until He sent David, and until He sent Jesus. Now that Jesus has come there is still a pattern of decline and renewal in the church. However there are some contrasts between then and now. In the days of the judges the pattern of decline and renewal did not stop the steady deterioration of Israel. The times of decline were more powerful than the renewals! There is reason to think it will be different in the days of the new covenant. The renewing work of God will be greater than the times of declension! Meanwhile God still tests His people. All around us are pagan peoples – whether sophisticated and scientific or primitive and weird. God still looks to see whether we will compromise with the religious ideas of the world, accompanied as they are by much wickedness. Or will we break the pattern and show that God's times of renewal will lift the church higher than it could ever go in the days of the judges. A greater Saviour is here, greater than Barak, greater than Samson. God's rescuings will be more powerful than ever. Meanwhile He still has ways of testing our allegiance.

# Chapter 4

## Odd People and an Odd Weapon
### (Judges 3:5–31)

Judges 3:5–16:31 is the central section of our book. The narrator has told of the origin of chaos and idolatry in Israel (1:1–3:4) and of the judges that God raised up to preserve the nation. Now in 3:5–16:31 he tells the stories of various judges. The are fourteen main characters: Othniel (3:7–11), Ehud (3:12–30), Shamgar (3:31), Deborah and Barak (4:1–5:31), Gideon (6:1–8:32), Abimelech (8:33–9:57), Tola (10:1–2), Jair (10:3–5), Jephthah (10:6–12:7), Ibzan (12:8–10), Elon (12:11–12), Abdon (12:13–15), and Samson (13:1–16:31).

First we have three principles.

1. **God never lets His people decline beyond recovery; eventually He sends rescuers**. Just as there is a principle of decline in the church, there is a principal of loyalty to His people in God! The church declines; God restores.

2. **The restoration generally came through individuals**. God would raise up these 'judges' to come to the aid of Israel and bring them back to God. If we wish to be used by God we have to be somewhat – not too much! – individualistic. God gives His people 'saviours' to work with them. I do not mean to deny the value of 'teamwork', but God's 'saviours' have a mind of their own. They stand against the trend and they call people back to God. They take actions in withstanding the successes of paganism and overthrowing the enemies of God.

3. **New 'rescuers' are needed in each generation**. The people of God tend to wander like sheep. We stay loyal to God while the strong leader is around. As soon as he goes, we reveal our

amazing tendency to fall away from God. Soon we need rescuing again!

Next we have three judges: Othniel (3:7–11), Ehud (3:12–30), Shamgar (3:31).

1. **Othniel was a man whose personal details are kept secret**. In the way in which the story is told, Othniel is a somewhat colourless rescuer for Israel; we know nothing about his personal character. There is probably a reason why the story of this first judge is told without any personal detail. God's restorations are more stories about God than stories about human heroes. God want us to learn about Himself more than about Othniel.

Israel's unfaithfulness arouses God's anger. For reasons that have already been explained, Israel was living among the Canaanites (3:5) and this soon led to idolatry (3:6). They worshipped false gods, following the customs of their pagan neighbours (3:7). This made God angry (3:8a) and the result was defeat for Israel at the hands of a king in the area north of them, in Aram-Naharaim. For eight years there was oppression by this king, whose name was Cushan-Rishathaim (3:8b).

God is eventually moved by His people's distress. The people cried to God and God answered (3:9).

God raises up a saviour. The particular way in which God answers the cries of His people is to send a person who will be able to help them. God likes to send people to help people. Othniel is God's gift to Israel at this time; he was Caleb's nephew (3:9).

The rescuer needed to have the power of the Holy Spirit. The Spirit of Yahweh came upon Othniel (3:10) and he went out to war against Cushan-Rishathaim. He did his work not simply by his own ability but by a special enabling of the Holy Spirit.

The outcome of victorious work for God was 'rest' (3:11). This is what 'entering into rest' is – it is the reward of one's labours after one has inherited the promises of God by diligent works of faith. 'Rest' is enjoyment of the blessings of God, the reward of diligent faith.

2. **Ehud was a man with a personal defect in his life**. Again Israel became careless; God allowed Moab to the south of

Israel to rise up in opposition against Israel (3:12). Moab had support from the Ammonites and the Amalekites (3:13). Israel's great victory of previous years was reversed. They lost 'the city of palm trees'. This was in the area when Jericho had existed and then had been destroyed. Years before the people of Israel had a mighty victory in this very area, near Jericho. Now the victory they had been famous for before, was reversed and they were failures in the very area where they had been a success before.

The people responded wisely. They had sinned badly and suffered for eighteen years (3:14) but they were brought by their sufferings to know what to do: they called upon God and asked for mercy (3:15a). God's answer to their plight was to send them a saviour – Ehud. He had a great weakness. His right hand was damaged and deformed and was quite unusable (3:15b).

God can use a person who has a personal defect in his life. Ehud was left handed. In ancient Israel where left-handedness was regarded as odd and even wicked, it would have meant that he had grown up as an odd character. But actually the very thing that was odd about Ehud was the thing God used. The Israelites had to send people to pay tribute to Eglon of Moab (3:15c). Ehud went as one of the people paying the tribute. He made a specially designed dagger (3:16). It was worn on the right side; it was not the place where one would look for daggers but Ehud was left-handed. It was long and thin. After the delegation had left, Ehud went back alone, pretending to have a special message for Eglon from God (3:17–19a). Eglon looked at Ehud; there was no weapon hanging at his left side. So he sent everyone out and waited for the message from Ehud's God. Ehud was speaking quietly. He had a secret message from God! Eglon arose to have Ehud whisper the message to him (3:19b–20). Then Ehud made use of his weakness, his left hand, and the long and thin dagger was put to good use as well (3:19b–22)! Soon Eglon was dead. Ehud made a quick but calm withdrawal (3:23). The servants waited long enough for him to escape (3:24–25). The Israelites were called to war (3:26–29) and Moab was defeated (3:30). Again the reward for faith was 'rest' (3:31). Ehud's 'deformity' was the very thing God used. On Ehud's part it took bold and confident faith that God would use the very thing about him which was his greatest weakness!

3. **Shamgar was a man with inadequate equipment** (3:31). We have seen that Ehud had a weakness in his body. Shamgar had a weakness in his equipment – but he used what he had. One man was odd; another man had an odd weapon. But God made His power obvious in human weakness.

# *Chapter 5*

## Barak, Hero of Faith

(Judges 4:1–24)

After the death of Ehud, Israel again fell into sin (4:1). Again they were chastised by God's sending an enemy into their lives (4:2). **Jabin** was the ruler of a city-state named Hazor. He had a general named **Sisera**. God gave His people into the hands of these two men and again Israel was forced to cry out in distress for God's intervention (4:3).

The person God raised up to be the deliverer of Israel was Barak, but first of all we are introduced to **Deborah,** She is 'judging' Israel at this time (4:4). She was a married lady and a prophetess. Unlike the previous judges she was not a military leader. Othniel was a judge who went to war (see 3:10). Ehud made a dagger for himself (see 3:15–21). Shamgar used an ox-goad (see 3:31), but what did Deborah use? She used a man – Barak!

Deborah's gift was skill in giving prophetic advice. Judges 4:6 brings us to **Barak**. Deborah used her prophetic gift to summon Barak and send him to war (4:6–7).

1. **Deborah is a gifted woman, but one who knows how to use her gift wisely and humbly**. Deborah is often quoted as an example of 'women's ministry' – and rightly so. She is a very unusual character in Israel's history. No other woman was so greatly used in the leadership of Israel. Her gift was the gift of speaking words of prophecy. 'Prophecy' is **speaking for God with words given by God**. The Bible makes it quite clear that women often are given the gift of prophecy and when they have such a gift they should use it. 'Your sons and daughters

shall prophesy' said Joel's prophecy quoted in Acts 2:17.
1 Corinthians 11:5 speaks of times when women will publicly
prophesy. The example of Agabus's daughters is well-known
(Acts 21:9).

Yet there is another side to this matter. It must be noted
how well Deborah worked with a man as the **military** leader of
Israel. Deborah gave to a man a prophetic word telling him
that he should be the military leader in this campaign against
Jabin and Sisera (4:6–7; see also 4:14). Later she will sing a
duet with Barak celebrating the victory (see 5:1). She worked
well and wisely with a male military leader.

2. **Barak is a man who works within the limits of his faith**.
The Bible tells us to use our gifts 'according to measure of
faith' (Romans 12:6; see also Ephesians 4:7). It is interesting
that in Hebrews 11:32 Barak is chosen as the hero of faith in
this story. But is important to note how his faith worked out
in practice.

A word came to Barak from God through Deborah (4:6–
7). It was a very bold and daring task that he was being called
to. Sisera had iron weapons and had ruled over Israel for
many years (see 4:3).

This is an important principle of faith. In the life of faith we
do as much as we dare do, and as much as God is calling us to
– but we stay within the limits of our faith. This is the point of
James 1:6–8. We ask God for what we can ask in total and
undoubting faith. When we venture into tasks about which we
are doubtful, we are unstable and we receive nothing from the
Lord.

It is the principle of Mark 11:22–24. When we ask for
God's help in bold and daring ventures we do so within the
limits of confident assured faith. 'Believe that what you say
will happen' – if you can! If in any particular task you **cannot**
speak in this way then realise you have come to a limit in the
faith you have. Faith is a 'measure', a 'portion' (Romans 12:6;
Ephesians 4:7).

Barak is a good example of this principle. 'If you go with
me, I will go', he said to Deborah, 'but if you do not go
with me, I won't go' (4:8). He was acting within his assurance.
He knew he could win this battle if he had Deborah's

encouragement. It is sometimes said that behind every great man is a great woman. I don't think this is always true. Jesus was unmarried; Paul was unmarried. They both had women helpers, but nothing is said of any special womanly encouragement in their lives. Job certainly got the wrong sort of encouragement from his wife (see Job 2:9)!

But Deborah provided womanly encouragement for Barak and Barak knew that he needed it, and was not afraid to say so!

However Deborah gives Barak a word of warning and (as it turns out) a prediction. If he takes Deborah with him, Barak will lose some of the glory for winning this particular victory over Israel's enemies. It will always be said that a woman was the one who brought the victory. But Barak does not worry about who will get the glory. He knows he has only limited faith. He knows he needs Deborah to give him encouragement in the battle. And he insists that she should go with him. This is what happens. Deborah and Barak go together into the battle (4:9b–10).

3. **This combination of ministries works well; the limited faith of Barak brings success**. Heber (4:11) is a fifth character in the story. His clan is a section of the Kenite tribe within Israel. They were a non-Israelite tribe, descendants of Moses' in-laws. Heber had a wife named Jael.

Sisera advanced to attack Israel (4:12–13). Deborah gave a powerful word of encouragement to Barak (4:14a). It was just what he needed. A great victory followed (4:14b–15a). Sisera fled for his life (4:15b). The enemy armies were destroyed (4:16) but Sisera ran to his non-Israelite friend Heber (4:17). But he was killed by Jael's wife (4:18–21). Deborah's word of prediction came true! Barak had to let the final glory for defeating Sisera go to a woman (4:22). But he was content with that, and soon the Israelites totally freed themselves from Jabin's domination (4:23–24). The victory was won by faith; Hebrews 11:32 regards Barak as the hero of faith – but it was won by faith working within the limits of assurance.

# Chapter 6

# Praising Our Victorious God

(Judges 5:1–10)

Deborah and Barak triumphed over the powerful city-state of Hazor, with its ruler Jabin and its military general Sisera. After the victory comes music and song, *'Then sang Deborah and Barak the son of Abinoam on that day:...'* (5:1). It reminds us of the song of Moses ('Then Moses and the people of Israel sang this song...' – Exodus 15:1). This is always the way it is when God's people get a victory; it turns to jubilation and music and singing. The people of God have something to sing about! Singing has to have a stimulus. For some it is wine that gets them going. For the people of God it is the mighty actions of God in our lives, in which He does unexpected things and delivers us from every kind of enemy. Singing is part of the fullness of the Holy Spirit (Ephesians 5:19). If God has done something mighty for us and we are full of spiritual joy, it bursts out of our heart in one way or another. When the prodigal comes home, when the Pharaohs and the Siseras that are against us are defeated, when persecutors outside of us or sinful ways within us are overthrown, there will be music and song.

1. **When God acts, many people get drawn into what God is doing**. In this song Deborah rejoices in the way in which many people got involved in the defeat of Jabin and his armies. Many of the 'princes' of Israel, the various tribal leaders, had been willing to get involved in this battle with Sisera.

*'The leaders took the lead in Israel.*
*The people volunteered to go into battle.*
*Praise be to Yahweh!'* (5:2).

The people had willingly offered themselves. This is always a mark of the blessing of God. When God's people 'offer themselves freely' (as Psalm 110:2 puts it) it is a cause for great rejoicing.

Deborah calls upon everyone to praise God for His mighty interventions.

> *'Listen, kings.*
> *Pay attention, rulers!*
> *I myself will sing to Yahweh.*
> *I will make music to Yahweh,*
>     *the God of Israel'* (5:3).

2. **When God acts, it is like a repetition of His salvation**. Deborah rejoices in the way in which God had acted on behalf of His people. It was as if God travelled from Sinai where He had made Israel into a holy nation. It is inspiring when God hears our prayers and meets our needs and steps in to bless His people in a dramatic way. Deborah compares it to what God had done when He first saved Israel.

> *'Yahweh, in the past you came from Seir.*
> *You marched out from the region of Edom,*
> *The earth shook; the skies rained.*
> *The clouds dropped water* (5:4).
> *The mountains shook before Yahweh,*
>     *the One who comes from Sinai,*
> *They shook before Yahweh, the God of Israel'* (5:5).

God acted for His people! 'Will not Yahweh go out before you', Deborah said to Barak (4:14). Yahweh came dramatically to rescue Israel in their battle with Sisera. The poet sees God as coming from the south, like someone who had travelled from Egypt or Mount Sinai. It was as if God had come from Mount Sinai to rescue His people in their battle. God arrived from Edom (also called Seir) which was to the south of Israel. The appearing of God from the south was a reminder of what God had done in defeating Pharaoh and leading the people to the land of Canaan (see Deuteronomy 33:2). The description recalls Moses' song in Deuteronomy 33 when God was also said to come from Edom (see Deuteronomy 33:2). Something similar is found in Habakkuk's psalm (see Habakkuk 3:3).

When God comes the very earth responds to Him. It shakes at His presence and the weather does what God wants it to. In the battle against Sisera, the defeat of the armies of Hazor was evidently helped by torrential rain: 'The skies rained; the clouds dropped water'.

3. **When God acts, situations change dramatically**. Deborah rejoices in the great changes that came in the nation when God sent her as a rescuer for the land.

*'In the days of Shamgar, son of Anath,*
*in the days of Jael, the main roads were empty.*
*Travellers kept to the winding pathways'* (5:6).

It was difficult for everyone in the days when Israel was dominated by its enemies. Bandits roamed the country; people were afraid to travel. Convoys of people selling their goods no longer felt free to move through the land.

*'Village life in Israel ceased...'*

Agricultural productiveness was reduced when raiders were endlessly attacking the farms. Then God sent rescuers: Shamgar, Jael, and especially Deborah!

*'Village life in Israel ceased,*
*it ceased until I, Deborah, arose.*
*I arose to be a mother in Israel'* (5:7).

Deborah is honest about the cause of the suffering of Israel.

*'At that time they chose to follow new gods.*
*Because of this, enemies fought us at our city gates.*
*No one could find a shield or a spear*
*among the forty thousand men of Israel'* (5:8).

It was idolatry that that brought Israel's defeat upon them. Then when the enemy appeared at the gates of the various towns of Israel, the people had no iron equipment with which to fight back.

This is the way it often is with God's dealings with His people. He allows them to be defeated. He lets them be almost totally overrun by their enemies. And then just at the point where you think the people of God are about to be exterminated altogether, God sends a rescuer. It has happened many times in the story of the church. After God's rescue everything is changed, and the life of the church begins to flow with energy once again.

*'My heart is with commanders of Israel.*
*They were willing volunteers among the people.*
*Praise be to Yahweh'* (5:9).

Deborah herself had rejoiced to see the leaders and the people together rousing themselves to get involved in rescuing the nation.

*'Tell out the story!*
*You who ride on white donkeys,*
*sitting on your saddle blankets,*
*and you who walk along the road'* (5:10).

Deborah wants everyone to know about this. 'Tell out the story!' 'You who ride on white donkeys' must refer to the leaders of the land. 'You who walk along the road' refers to the ordinary people. Everyone must praise God for the marvellous victory He has given His people.

This is what it is like when God acts to restore and revive His people. There is a new unity, a new certainty that God is at work, and the church of God is dramatically lifted out of its defeat and weakness.

# Chapter 7

## Involvement in God's Kingdom

(Judges 5:11–31)

One major concern of Deborah's song is to note who did and who did not get involved in zeal for the kingdom of God.

1. **Deborah is concerned about involvement in worship**. She summons everyone to praise God, including the rich ('You who ride on white donkeys . . .') and the common people ('you who walk along the roads'). The next lines refer to the shepherds.

> 'Listen to the sound of the singers
> at the watering places.
> There they tell about the victories of Yahweh.
> They tell about the victories of Yahweh's warriors in
> Israel.
> There was a time when Yahweh's people
> went down to the city gates' (5:11).

When Sisera's invaders had attacked the land, life had become difficult for the shepherds. They had been forced to shelter inside the towns with walls and gates around them Now at the various watering places where the shepherds take their sheep, musicians should assemble to lead the shepherds in praising God.

Deborah knows that she too must praise God. Worship of Yahweh is not just for shepherds.

> 'Wake up, wake up, Deborah!
> Wake up, wake up, sing a song!'

And she calls upon her friend Barak.

> 'Get up, Barak!
> Son of Abinoam, lead away your captives!' (5:12)

2. **Deborah is concerned about involvement in exertion and struggle**. She records those who were and those who were not involved in rescuing the nation.

> *'Then a remnant of the nobles went down* [1]
> *The people of Yahweh went down as mighty warriors'*
> (5:13).

She notes again that both high-born leaders ('a remnant of the nobles') and the common people ('the people of Yahweh') were working together.

Then she notes which tribes got involved and which did not.

> *'Some came from **Ephraim**, whose home is in Amalek*
> *After you, **Benjamin**, with your people!*
> *From the family group of **Makir**, the commanders came down.*
> *And from **Zebulun** came men who lead with an officer's staff'* (5:14).

First, four tribes are mentioned which helped in the battle, Ephraim who occupied territory once occupied by Amalekites (Judges 12:15), Benjamin who had a position of leadership, Makir which was part of the tribe of Manasseh, and Zebulun.

Another supportive and loyal tribe is mentioned.

> *'The princes of **Issachar** were with Deborah.*
> *The people of Issachar were loyal to Barak.*
> *They followed him into the valley'* (5:15a).

But next is mentioned a tribe which refused to come to the aid of the whole nations.

> *'The sections of **Reubenites** thought hard about what they would do* (5:15b).
> *Why did you stay by the sheepfold?*
> *Was it to hear the music played for your sheep?*
> *The Reubenites thought hard about what they would do'*
> (5:16).

Deborah is being sarcastic! Three other unsupportive sections of the people were the inhabitants of Gilead, the people of Dan, and the people of Asher.

> *'The people of **Gilead** stayed east of the Jordan River.*
> *People of **Dan**, why did you stay by the ships?*
> *The people of **Asher** stayed at the seashore*
> *They stayed at their safe harbours'* (5:17).

The people of Gilead thought they need not join in the
conflict since they live on the other side of the Jordan river.
The people of Dan were too busy doing business with
Phoenicians and their ships. The people of Asher were unwilling to leave their homes by the Mediterranean sea.

Two peoples who were very different were Zebulun and
Naphtali.

> '*But the people of* **Zebulun** *risked their lives.*
> *So did the people of* **Naphtali** *on the battlefield'*
>     (5:18).

Deborah puts their deeds into song. These tribes will have
their successes named wherever this song is sung.

God is looking for involvement in God's kingdom, and that
includes support of His leaders. Deborah has mentioned, in
one way or another, all of the tribes of Israel except the
Levites. She has recorded forever those who will receive
honour for what they did, and all of those who deserve a
reputation for neglect of God's kingdom, laziness, preoccupa-
tion with their own business – even enjoyment of the
Mediterranean seaside!

3. **The matter of involvement brings cursing for some and
honour for others**. The battle was intense, but the kings of
Canaan were thoroughly defeated.

> '*The kings came, and they fought.*
> *At that time the kings of Canaan fought*
> *at Taanach, by the waters of Megiddo.*
> *But they took away no silver or possessions of Israel'*
>     (5:19).

But God was in control of what happened and even the
stars and the rivers were against His enemies. Deborah
envisages the stars watching the battle and giving their
encouragement. Torrential rain helped Israel and the flood-
waters of the rivers hindered Sisera's men.

> '*The stars fought from heaven.*
> *From their paths, they fought Sisera* (5:20).
> *The Kishon river swept Sisera's men away,*
> *that old river, the Kishon River.*
> *March on, my soul, with strength!'* (5:21)

Then Sisera's forces tried to escape.

'They the horses' hoofs beat the ground
Galloping, galloping to Sisera's mighty horses' (5:22).

It was at this time that one town refused to give any help to Israel.

'"May the town of Meroz be cursed" said the angel of the Lord.
"Bitterly curse its people,
because they did not come to help the Lord.
They did not fight the strong enemy"' (5:23).

But Jael is ever to be remembered as a woman who supported the people of God.

'May Jael, the wife of Heber the Kenite,
be blessed above all women who live in tents (5:24).
Sisera asked for water
but Jael gave him milk.
In a bowl fit for a ruler
she brought him cream (5:25).
Jael reached out and took the tent peg.
Her right hand reached for the workman's hammer.
And she hit Sisera! She smashed his head!
She crushed and pierced the side of his head (5:26)!
At Jael's feet he sank.
He fell, and he lay there.
At her feet he sank. He fell.
Where Sisera sank, there he fell, dead!' (5:27)

At the end of the battle, all expectations have been reversed. The people of Jabin were confident of victory. Sisera's mother takes it for granted that her son will return victorious.

'Sisera's mother looked out through the window.
She looked through the curtains.
She asked, "Why is Sisera's chariot so late in coming?
Why are the sounds of his chariot's horses delayed?"
(5:28).
The wisest of her servant ladies answer her.
And Sisera's mother says to herself, (5:29)
"Surely they are taking the possessions of the people they defeated!
Surely they are dividing those things among themselves!
A girl or two is being given to each soldier.

> *Maybe Sisera is taking pieces of dyed cloth.*
> *Maybe they are even taking*
> *pieces of dyed, embroidered cloth for my neck,*[2]
> *as plunder"'* (5:30).

There has been joy for Israel but tragedy for Sisera's mother. This is the way it will be for the future of the kingdom of God. The expectations of the wicked will be entirely reversed.

Deborah's conclusion follows.

> *'Let all your enemies die this way, Lord!*
> *But let all the people who love you*
> *be powerful like the rising sun!'*

And a final comment on the story of Deborah and Barak tells of the result of their work. *'So there was peace in the land for forty years'* (5:31).

## Notes

[1] This translation reads *yarad* instead of *yerad* and ignores the Hebrew accents which puts 'people' in the previous line.

[2] This translation slightly emends the Hebrew.

# Chapter 8

## Gideon's Call

(Judges 6:1–24)

For the fourth time Israel sinned, and God handed them over to their enemies, this time to the Midianites (6:1).

God chastens His people's sins. The familiar pattern of sin-followed-by-chastening continued in Israel (see 3:7, 12; 4:1). Once again Israel's predicament was a desperate one. The Israelites were hiding in caves (6:2). Their enemies would invade at the time when Israel were sowing their seed. Then (since some small amount of seed was planted despite the attacks) they would attack again at harvest time (6:3). It was a deliberate policy, full of hatred, designed to reduced Israel to extreme poverty and weakness. When the Midianites invaded, Amalekites and other eastern people joined in. Together the enemies came in vast numbers to devastate the land (6:4–5); Israel was in a joyless and distressing situation. It was God's way of putting pressure on the people to get them to pray (6:6). When we slip into prayerlessness God is able to drive us to prayer. Our troubles exert pressure on us and might lead us to pray as never before.

God prepares the way for restoration by sending prophecy. The nation's turning to idolatry has been mentioned three times before (3:7–11, 12–30, 31; 4:1–5:31) and we may assume something similar happened in the days of Shamgar (3:31). On those four occasions God simply rescued them, but now He first sends a prophet (6:7). Chastening is of no value if it is not interpreted. Actually the prophet does not rebuke them very powerfully. God simply reminds them of what He has

37

done. He delivered them from bondage, released them from oppression and gave them Canaan (6:8–9). He wished them to show their gratitude by not worshipping the gods of the Amorites who lived in Canaan. But they did not heed God's demand (6:10). They are sinning against grace, sinning against His amazing mercy.

God eventually raises up a rescuer; God calls Gideon. God's instrument is an undistinguished person going about his regular duties (6:11). An angel appears. It is 'the angel of the Lord', the angel who specially represents Yahweh himself. Gideon has taken his wheat to a winepress, a hollow in the ground, where he hopes that he will not be discovered by any invading Midianites. Normally a farmer would take wheat to be threshed out into the open countryside, but the Midianite danger made that impossible.

1. **When God calls us He treats us not as we are but as we shall be**. God treats Gideon not as he is but as the military hero that he will be. The angel speaks to Gideon, *'Yahweh is with you, you mighty warrior'* (6:12)! Actually Gideon seems to be anything but a mighty warrior! He is hiding from Midianites. He is perplexed and resentful about Israel's sufferings (6:13). He is sceptical, reckoning God has simply abandoned Israel (6:14).

God reckons Gideon to be a mighty man of valour. Actually he is not that yet, but he will be and God is dealing with Gideon not in terms of what he is but in terms of what he will be.

2. **When God calls us He treats us totally in grace**. God's call disregarded Gideon's sinfulness. Gideon was quite rebellious and cynical in the way in which he answered God. He was in a bitter mood. But God took no notice of that whatsoever. We are 'called with a holy calling' but it is 'not because of anything we have done but because of his own purpose and grace' (2 Timothy 1:9)

Salvation comes to us in the same way. When we trust in Jesus, God says 'I pronounce you righteous'. We are actually not righteous in ourselves at the time God saves us, but God looks ahead to what we shall be eventually. In heaven we shall be totally sinless. But when we come to faith in Jesus God reckons that righteousness as ours straightaway. 'Justification' is God's treating us not as we are but as we shall be.

3. **We may know we are being called by God when we find God steadily insisting on His will**. God does not argue with Gideon. When God's call comes to us we find that God is gently compelling. *'Go in the strength you have and save Israel ... Am I not sending you?'* (6:14). Gideon does not feel he has much strength. He is hoping no Midianites will find him in his winepress. But God's call is enough. 'Go in the strength you have' says God.

4. **When God calls us He disregards weakness**. Gideon feels inferior and weak. Manasseh is not known for its military heroism. Gideon's clan is the weakest in Manasseh. And Gideon is the weakest person in his family (6:15)! It does not matter to God. God still insists that Gideon must be the rescuer. The enemies of Israel, the Midianites, will be thoroughly defeated in a single event (6:16).

5. **When God's call comes, the beginning of the work is to be at peace with Him**. God's assurance begins with Gideon's asking for a miraculous sign. 'If you really are choosing me to do this work, show me by some kind of sign that you really are sent from God', he asks (6:17). He wants the angel to accept a sacrifice (6:18). He goes and prepares a meal (6:19). The angel tells him where to put the meal (6:20). Then He consumes the meal and disappears from sight (6:21). Gideon is stunned. He has seen God and is it well-known that no one can see God and live (6:22). But it is alright. He has not seen the fullness of God's glory; the angel has been visually representing God in a way that is safe for Gideon. Gideon is reassured that there is peace between him and God (6:23). Gideon builds an altar (6:24). The place became known as 'Yahweh Shalom', 'the LORD is peace'.

There is no blessing in serving God unless it begins with our being personally reconciled to Him. Such peace with God comes with a sacrifice – the blood of our Lord Jesus Christ. The 'the LORD is peace' for us, and we are ready to serve Him.

## Chapter 9

# Early Steps of Faith

(Judges 6:25–40)

Gideon was a weak person. He could get into moods of scepticism and doubt. He could be almost overcome with unbelief.

1. **One way God had of training Gideon was to give him practice in a smaller venture of faith before giving him the bigger venture of faith**. God gradually brought Gideon up to a high level of faith. Gideon himself is one of the weakest believers there ever was! His first reaction to God's call was one of scepticism and unbelief – and throughout his story he is prone to lapses into unbelief.

God helps Gideon to come to a higher level of faith by giving him something smaller to do at first. He is asked to break down his father's altar (6:25). He had already built one altar. Now God asks him to build a second altar. He must take a bull from his father's herd, break down his father's altar and build an altar of worship for Yahweh on his father's farm. Then he must sacrifice his father's bull (6:26). It would be a dangerous thing to do. To tear down an altar to Baal – the god of fertility – at a time when everyone was worshipping Baal was to ask for trouble. His father was a Baal-worshipper; there was not much chance that his father would be pleased to discover what Gideon had done.

Gideon did as he was told (6:27), but he did it in the middle of the night when nobody was around to see what he was doing! Well, almost nobody! Actually he made use of ten servants. Asking ten men to keep a secret like that was to ask the impossible. The next day it does not take long to find out who it was who had broken down the altar to Baal and replaced it with an altar to Yahweh (6:28–29). Soon the men of the town were threatening to kill Gideon (6:30).

God honours Gideon's faith. At this point God does something unexpected for Gideon. The first Baalite idolater he won round to the worship of Yahweh was his own father! The one he had feared so much (see 6:15, 27) actually turns around and supports his son. He was obviously a powerful and influential man. Even Gideon was afraid of him. But he is unexpectedly won over to the cause of Yahweh. 'Let Baal defend himself!' says Gideon's father (6:31). When we honour God, God honours us. Gideon learns that when he takes a step of faith – however fearful he might be at the time – God will honour him and unexpected blessings are likely to follow. Gideon gets a new name (6:32). He becomes known as Jerub-Baal ('Let Baal contend!'). It would be a permanent reminder to Gideon that Yahweh could change situations. 'Let Baal contend' if he can – but he can't!

So Gideon has been given a small step of faith to take. It prepares him and trains him to do greater things for God.

2. **God is gracious to Gideon's 'sign-seeking'**. Gideon is so afraid that he might do something wrong or take a false step. He has already (see 6:17) once asked God to give him a special sign to confirm that what he is doing is authentic. Now he does the same thing again.

The Midianites and their friends assemble at the valley of Jezreel, a valley in the north of Israel branching westwards off of the Jordan valley through which the River Jordan runs (6:33). Gideon receives a fresh empowering from the Holy Spirit. He summons the Abiezrites, the people of the area around Ophrah (6:34). Then he called for help from three of Israel's tribes, the tribes of Asher, Zebulun, and Naphtali (6:35). At that point Gideon again gets nervous. Hundreds of people are now looking to him as their leader. He has summoned them. Will he be able to lead them into victory? Once again, Gideon feels very doubtful, and again he asks for sign. First he asks for a miraculous sign that God really is about to give him success. He asks God to arrange for a fleece of wool to be wet with dew while the ground around is dry (6:36–37). God answers and Gideon gets the sign that he wants (6:38a). But still he is not satisfied. This is the trouble with sign-seeking. Once you ask for one you want another to make you sure about the first one! So Gideon asks for the sign to be the other way around. The fleece is to be dry and the ground around is to be wet with dew (6:39). Again God answers, and Gideon is given what he wants (6:40).

1. God will often refuse to give unbelievers a sign. An evil and adulterous generation seek a sign but no sign shall be given them except the resurrection of Jesus Himself. Jesus Himself is the sign for those without any faith at all.

2. Yet when weak believers need help, God might be willing to confirm His will by giving something that doubly demonstrates what His will is. God answered Gideon's requests for a sign, and gave him what he asked for. This is not a sign of how strong Gideon is; it is a sign of how weak he is! God sees that Gideon is so weak that he needs a sign; so He lets Gideon have what he needs.

3. When God does confirm His will it puts the Christian under heavy responsibility. When we have the word of God and something in addition to the Word of God, then our responsibility to obey it is heavy indeed. We are in a very serious situation if God makes doubly clear to us what His will is. To whom much is given, much is required. If God makes doubly clear what His will is, we must be doubly eager to obey it.

# Chapter 10

# Preparing for Victory
(Judges 7:1–23)

Gideon has accepted the fact that God is calling him to be the deliverer of Israel. He has asked God for various signs to prove that he is indeed in God's will. God has answered him and given him his requests. Now the battle is soon to begin. God gets the soldiers ready for victory; then He gets Gideon ready for victory.

1. **First there is the preparation of the soldiers**. Gideon sets up his camp at En Harod, a place where there is a spring of water not far from the valley of Jezreel (7:1a). The camp of the mighty Midianite army is not very far away to the north (7:1b). Gideon's army numbers about 32,000 men. But then God gives Gideon some surprising guidance.

**God wants to use people who are weak**. God tells Gideon, *'The people with you are too many...'* (7:2). God does not want the people to be so numerically powerful that, after the battle is finished, they take the credit of victory for themselves.

**God wants to use people who are willing**. Anyone who wants to go home may go home (7:3)! Gideon must tell the people plainly, 'Anyone who is afraid may go!' About 22,000 men go home! The remaining 10,000 men are ones who want to be there. They will not go home even when they are given permission to do so. Jesus still wants a family of disciples consisting of those who are willing to do God's will (see Mark 3:31–35). He says 'If anyone wishes to come after me...'. It is a personal matter: 'If anyone...'. It is a voluntary matter: 'If anyone wishes...'. So Gideon said to his men, 'If you feel

43

afraid and you want to go home, you may go...'. Maybe some who stayed were afraid too, but they were unwilling to go home. Gideon himself was fearful, as we shall see.

**God wants to use people who are watchful**. The numbers were still too large; God wanted even fewer. Gideon is told to take them down to the place where the springs of fresh water are to be found (7:4). There He will give further instructions about who is to go on this campaign against the Midianites. Anyone who drinks water by lapping up the water in dog-like fashion (apparently from a cupped hand) is to be put on one side. They are the ones God will use. Anyone who drinks water by getting down on all fours is to be allowed to go home. The ones who scoop up water and drink it from a cupped hand are the ones God wants to use. By this test the number that God will use is reduced to three hundred men (7:5–7).

Is there any significance in the way the two groups drink water? I am sure the main point is simply that God wanted to reduce the number to a smaller group. They did not have to be great military heroes or skilful soldiers. On the other hand there surely was a reason why one group of soldiers drank water in one way, and a smaller group drank water in another way. Of course, all of the soldiers were thirsty. All of them needed to quench their thirst. One group gets down on all fours to quench their thirst. Nothing matters to them but having a long, long guzzle, from the water-spring.

The other group have something else on their minds as well as their own needs. They remember that there are Midianites not far away who might attack at any moment. They are not about to put down their weapons and quench their thirst on all fours. They also are keeping in mind what could happen at any moment. They are not so eager to meet their needs of a thirst-quenching drink that they forget to keep themselves ready for an attack from the Midianites.

It is a parable of the kind of people God wants to use. They may not be super-saints, but they are people who are less concerned with the pleasures and needs of life and more concerned about what is happening in the Lord's kingdom. They do not 'guzzle on all fours' and neglect God's kingdom.

Rather they take small sips from cupped hands and while they do so, they stay wide-awake to what is happened in the work of God. The three hundred take the provisions of those who go home (7:8).

2. **Next there is the preparation of Gideon**. One might think that Gideon would by now be ready for the conflict again Midian, but Gideon still has some doubts. He is still a man who needs God's help.

**Gideon has to admit to himself that he is still a man with weakness**. Once again Gideon needs a sign! God tells him that the day for victory has arrived (7:9). But, says God, if Gideon is still afraid he can creep down to the enemy camp and he will hear something that will encourage him (7:10–11). It must be noticed that God's offer requires that Gideon admits to himself that he still has a problem with needless fear.

**God helps Gideon to rise to fearless assurance**. The number of the enemy is vast (7:12). Gideon is allowed to hear a man relating a dream. One little loaf of bread rolls into the camp. It is small yet it knocks down a large tent (7:13). His friend recognizes the symbolism of the dream. The small loaf of barley bread stands for Gideon. The large tent stands for the Midianites (7:14). It encourages Gideon and brings him to a complete assurance that God is about to work (7:15).

3. **When God has done his work of preparation, the tiny army are given an effortless victory**. Gideon divides the three hundred into three (7:16). This will have the effect of spreading them out and giving the impression that there is a large army. The soldiers must imitate Gideon when they get to the edge of the enemy camp (7:17) and at the right time shout *'For the LORD and for Gideon'* (7:18).

They arrive at a time when the enemy camp are likely to be deeply asleep (7:19). They have trumpets ready and lamps burning beneath earthenware pots. Suddenly they uncover the lights and start blowing on the trumpets and shouting (7:20). The enemy army are suddenly woken up from their sleep. The Israelites do not have to do anything; they simply stand where they are! They stand still and see God's salvation. Without the three hundred having to do any fighting, the enemy armies panic. In their confused state they start killing each other!

Then they run for their lives (7:21–22). The men from the three tribes are summoned for the final triumph (7:23; see 6:35). A tiny army won a mighty victory because God gave the success to them.

# Chapter 11

# 'Human ... Just Like Us'
## (Judges 7:24–8:21)

Gideon was always 'a human being just like us' (as James might have put it – see James 5:17). His strength was made perfect in his weakness. Sometimes he is a wise leader; sometimes he is a man of obvious weakness and inclined to make precisely the kind of mistakes we might ourselves have made. At first, he shows himself to be a man of wisdom but soon his weaknesses appear.

1. **He was able to give a soft answer in a time of criticism**. When the Midianites ran to escape what they thought was Gideon's mighty army, they ran in the direction of the Ephraimites whose territory was to the south of Gideon's own tribe of Manasseh. Since they were running in that direction, Gideon asked for the help of the people of Ephraim, in addition to the three tribes who were already involved in the battle. They were in a position to guard the river-crossings and so they were able to kill two of the escaping generals of the Midianite army (7:24–25). But it leads to some complaint. The Ephraimites were bitterly critical of Gideon for not having called upon their help earlier (8:1). Gideon could have reacted violently (as Jephthah did on a similar occasion in later years – Judges 12:1–6) but he chose to preserve the peace by not reacting with a violent spirit. He simply pointed to the major part that Ephraim had played in the final victory. They had defeated two of the enemy's generals (8:2–3).

2. **He was able to show great determination when others had no faith in him**. Gideon and his three hundred men gave chase

after two Midianite kings. They were weary and so asked the help of the people of Succoth (8:4–5). But the people of Succoth had no faith in Gideon's small army (8:6). Gideon however was quite confident he would defeat the two kings; then he would return to punish those who would put no faith in him but wanted to wait until his victory was so obvious no faith was needed (8:7). Something similar happened at Peniel (8:8–9).

Gideon had faith in God ('... Yahweh has given Zebah and Zalmunna ...') and therefore faith in himself ('... into my hand ...'). At a time when no one believed in the victory that was to be given him, Gideon was still confident because he was confident in God.

3. **He was able to persevere to the very end of what he was being called to do**. The Midianites were now severely reduced in number. Only fifteen thousand were left; a hundred and twenty thousand had perished (8:10). Gideon continues to press his advantage to the very end, attacking the armies while they are off-guard, pursuing their leaders, and reducing the enemy armies to chaos (8:11–12).

Gentleness, determination, perseverance. These are the last times we shall have cause to admire Gideon. For the rest of his story, he appears in his weaknesses rather than in the strengths that arose from his faith.

1. It soon appears that there is **a strand of ruthlessness** in Gideon's character that now begins to show itself. He returns from battle (8:13) and compels a young man to write for him the names of the officials and elders of Succoth (8:14). Soon he scourged the elders of Succoth with thorns and briars (8:15). Then he destroyed the a tower in Peniel as he said he would (8:16; see 8:8–9) and then went further still killing the men of the city (8:17). The man who once had thought himself not to be a 'mighty man of valour' has now become too confident in himself and has moved from indecisiveness to arrogance.

2. Also **a strand of vindictiveness** appears in Gideon's character in his dealings with Zebah and Zalmunna. When he finally corners these two Midianite kings, he kills them not because of their enmity to God, but in revenge for the killing

of his own brothers (8:18–19). Gideon even wants his own young son to have a part in taking family-revenge against the men who killed those who were Gideon's brothers and Jether's uncles (8:20). At one time Gideon did not think himself to be a mighty man of valour and was afraid of his own father (see 6:12, 27). Now he expects a younger boy to have greater courage than he had when he was that age! It seems that Gideon is getting increasingly ambitious to have a family who aspire to be military heroes and rulers in Israel. As we shall see, in addition to Jether he has a son named 'My father is king' (Abi-melech)! Gideon was generous and wise in dealing with the people of Ephraim but he is never seen being merciful at any later stage of his story.

His son is unable to kill his uncle's murderers. Gideon's enemies scornfully tell him to do the job himself – and he does (8:21).

Scarcely ever in the Bible do we find that the heroes of faith have an unblemished record. Many of them start out well but deteriorate towards the end of their lives. Anyone who reads much in the historical books of the Old Testament finds again and again that the people he or she begins to admire turn out to be disappointing. Every institution, every character, every king, every man or woman of faith turns out to be fallible and imperfect. There is only one Person in the Bible who never fails and never disappoints and that is Jesus. Only one Person really did endure to the end with an unblemished record. Only one Person really deserved to be our hero, the Lord Jesus Christ. Gideon's strong point was not anything in himself. He had one strong point – his faith in a strong Saviour-God.

Yet there is something encouraging in all of this. If God can use fallible people like Gideon, then God can use me and God can use you. And if Gideon's faith challenges us to be a 'mighty person of valour', his weakness might challenge us to hate vindictiveness and leave revenge to God.

# *Chapter 12*

# Privilege Without Responsibility

## (Judges 8:22–35)

Gideon tended always to underestimate what God could do in his life. The time comes when Gideon receives a fresh challenge to serve God. The people of Israel ask Gideon to start a line of kings in Israel. 'You have saved us; so now we want you and your descendants to be a line of kings to rule the nation' (see 8:22). One part of their request is reasonable. Someone who has shown that he is able to be a Saviour is likely to be a good man to have as a king.

Jesus is in fact the only One to whom this line of argument really applies. 'Saviour ... therefore ruler' applies to Him alone. He alone is unchangingly faithful. He is eternal and while it is progressing, never hands over His work to anyone else.

However there is another part of the people's request which is foolish. The idea that a **line** of kings will help them is foolish. Will the son of a saviour equally be a saviour?

What should Gideon have done at this point? There are three possibilities. (i) He could have simply turned down the offer and thrown off all further responsibility for Israel. (ii) He could have accepted the offer and then he and his descendants would have been a line of kings in Israel. However there could be no way that he could guarantee that his sons and grandsons would be worthy as kings of Israel. (iii) The wisest course of action would have been to take some kind of middle course. He could have simply retained his position as a kind of permanent judge, and then left it to God as to what should happen when his reign was at an end.

What Gideon did was to turn down the offer, but then to live like a king without taking responsibility for the future well-being of the nation. He declines the offer, saying *'Yahweh will rule over you'* (8:23). So far, so good. Yet from that point onward Gideon made mistakes. He no longer sought ways of serving his nation. Yet at the same time he wanted the privileges that arose from his almost being a king in Israel.

There are times when we turn down the offer of something we know would be wrong but then we hanker after the very thing we have said 'no' to! Gideon says 'no' to the offer of kingship – and yet much that he does afterwards is behaving like a dynastic king. And Gideon himself must take some of the blame if later one of his sons, Abimelech, tried to become a king. After all, 'Abimelech' means 'My father is king!'

1. **It was a mistake to seek wealth without responsibility.** When the people asked Gideon to start a line of kings in Israel, Gideon used the opportunity to ask for gold (8:24). Kings were famous for accumulating gold. The law of Israel warned any king 'He must not accumulate large amounts of silver and gold' (Deuteronomy 17:17). Gideon says 'no' to kingship, but then immediately starts acting like a king – but not a good one! He wants the money but he is not doing much to help Israel.

2. **It was a mistake to take a step towards idolatry.** Gideon is given the gold that he wants (8:25–26). The people each give a piece of gold from what they had taken from the Midianites. Then Gideon uses it to make his home town, Ophrah, into a kind of religious sanctuary. He makes a golden 'ephod'. The 'ephod' was some sort of coat in which stones were kept. When the stones were thrown down, they acted as dice, giving God's will. They could give one of three results: 'yes', 'no', or 'no answer'. Gideon had always had a problem being sure about God's calling. Now he makes Ophrah into a sacred city, where people will come to worship God and get guidance from Him. Its central spectacle is Gideon's ephod. Not only is

Gideon acting as an almost-king. He is acting as an almost-high-priest.

But none of this is following God's will. There is a tabernacle at Shiloh; God's true 'ephod' belongs to the great high-priest in the tribe of Levi. Gideon had made himself his own high-priest – in the line of Manasseh! Gideon said 'no' to the offer of kingship but now is acting as if he is king-and-priest combined. The people began worshipping the ephod; it brought idolatry into Gideon's family (8:27). The problem all began when Gideon was given an opportunity to be responsible for the nation of Israel. He turned down the responsibility, but he wanted the privileges.

3. **It was a mistake to set up a royal harem**. During Gideon's lifetime the Midianites were subdued, and there was a generation of peace (8:28). Gideon himself continued to act like a bad king. The Mosaic law had warned Israel against having a king who accumulated many wives. 'He must not take many wives' said Deuteronomy 17:17. Gideon says 'no' to kingship, but then he goes back to Ophrah (8:29) and starts living a life that resembles that of a king. He has many wives, many sons (8:30). He takes a concubine in Shechem (8:31) and has a son through her. The son's name is Abimelech, which means 'My father is king!' Gideon said 'no' to kingship, but then got as near to being a king as he could get! Near eastern kings paraded their status by taking many wives.

When Gideon died he was given an honourable burial (8:32) but then Israel went back to its sinful ways (8:33). They had not learned the lesson. The idolatry which brought them trouble in the first place (see 6:1) was taken up again. They forgot God (8:34) and they forgot Gideon and what he had done (8:35).

Gideon missed a great opportunity for good when Israel offered him kingship. The Mosaic law allowed Israel to have a king (see Deuteronomy 17:14–20). If they had consulted the Lord, perhaps he would have let them have Gideon as their king. If he had obeyed the rules about kingship in Deuteronomy 17:14–20 he might have upheld righteousness in Israel. He could have become a judge like Samuel, upholding righteousness.

Instead he acted like Solomon, collecting gold and wives, making his city into a religious sanctuary, but eventually leading Israel into idolatry. It is one thing to begin well; it is another thing to continue in faithfulness to the very end.

# *Chapter 13*

## Abimelech and Jotham
### (Judges 9:1–21)

Judges 9 is about Abimelech, but it is really continuing the
story of Gideon. These famous heroes of faith in the Book of
Judges are, as we have seen, very weak and fallible people.
Gideon made some bad mistakes in the later stage of his life,
and his blunders continued to have consequences in the next
generation. We have already been told of Gideon's concubine
who gave birth to Abimelech (see 8:31).

The sons of Gideon were acting as if they were a tribe of
kings! This made it possible for a man like Abimelech to
promote his own ambitions. Abimelech goes to the family of
his father's concubine and gets them to put a suggestion to the
people of Shechem. Would they rather be ruled by seventy
sons of Gideon or have one them – Abimelech! – to be a king
(9:1–2)? Gideon's sons are not popular. They are now all
acting like kings. Gideon's example is followed by all seventy
of his sons!

The citizens of Shechem chose to have Abimelech as their
leader (9:3). They provided him with money (9:4) and with his
new wealth Abimelech persuaded a gang of unscrupulous
delinquents to become his private army (9:4). He goes to
Ophrah, the home-town of Gideon and the centre of the
idolatry which had arisen because of Gideon's ephod (see
8:27). There, seeking to destroy any possible rivals, he
murdered all except one of his half-brothers (9:5). After he
thought all rivals were out of the way, the people of Shechem
arranged for his coronation (9:6).

But one half-brother had escaped! Jotham climbs partway up the 700 metre slope of Mount Gerizim. It is an area with unusual acoustical characteristics and had a natural platform overlooking the town of Shechem. Jotham began to shout a message; his voice sounded down the slopes of hillside. He probably shouted out who he was and people began to gather to listen to what he was saying (9:7). He tells the people a parable which hints at the worthlessness of Abimelech. The trees want a king. They invite the olive tree (9:8–9), the fig-tree (9:10–11) and the vine (9:12–13); but each of them turn down the offer of kingship. Then the trees invite the thorn-bush to be their king (9:14). The olive-tree, the fig-tree and the vine are reluctant to give up their good work (providing oil, fruit and wine). On the other hand the thorn-bush is virtually useless! Only trees which are desperate or simple-minded would look for a leader in a thorn-bush!

*'If you really want to anoint me king...'*, says the thorn bush. He knows that the trees would only turn to a thorn-bush if they were desperate! If they want such a worthless tree, the tree is willing! But on the other hand if they reject the thorn-tree, the worthless thorn-tree will then become angry and destroy even the mighty and impressive cedars of Lebanon (9:15). Now the trees have put their request to the thorn-tree, their future is a bleak and dismal one whether their request goes forward or not!

Jotham applies the parable to the people's choice of Abimelech. If they have done well in showing such ingratitude to the line of Gideon – all well and good (9:16–19). May they and Abimelech bring joy to each other! Like the thorn-tree Abimelech was the most worthless figure they could possibly have chosen for the task, but now they have chosen him they are in trouble. They have got a king who will cut and wound them. If they have been so unrighteous and cruel as to show such ingratitude towards Gideon (as they obviously have!), then may fiery destruction exterminate both them and their king (9:20)! At that point Jotham runs for his life and goes to stay in a town called Beer. He lives there with an uneasy anxiety about what vengeance Abimelech might arrange for him (9:21).

1. **Challenges to responsibility must be taken seriously**. The story of Abimelech throws light on Gideon's refusal to become king. Gideon might have arranged for an orderly line of kings. He might have trained one of his sons to be a righteous king over Israel. But enjoying an unofficial kingship, kingship without being king, he had the privileges of kingship but none of its responsibilities. He took no steps to secure the future. No doubt securing the future is not completely possible but Gideon did not make even the feeblest attempts to secure righteousness in the nation after his own lifetime. The result is that Gideon left a power-vacuum after his death, and one of the worst of his sons has stepped into the gap. But the blame must largely go to Gideon. He took no responsibility for Israel's future. Now one of his own offspring is bringing ruination to the land.

The lesson for us is: challenges to responsibility must be taken seriously. The offer of kingship that came to Gideon was the chance of a lifetime to achieve some good in Israel, in one way or another, but Gideon missed the opportunity.

2. **The neglect of the true leadership will lead to the rise of the unworthy leadership**. Gideon took no steps to secure a good future for the land of Israel. His sons were living like kings and there was dissatisfaction among the people. The question 'Do you want to be ruled by the seventy sons of Gideon?' had an obvious answer. 'No, we are not getting much blessing from these sons of Gideon'. There was an obvious gap in leadership, and where there is a gap in leadership, an unworthy person will arise to fill it.

Leaders have to be men and women of sincerity, ability, generosity. They have to have the needs of the people at heart. Where such leaders are missing, false teachers will arise. If Gideons are missing, Abimelechs will step in.

3. **There are times when one must boldly prepare for the future**. There was not much that this youngest son, Jotham, could do. He genuinely had the needs of the people on his heart. He could not remove Abimelech, but he could speak out, saying what needed to be said and announcing what inevitably would happen. The people's decision was like the choice of a thorn-bush. Abimelech's reign could do no good.

The sooner that was realised, the better. Jotham could at least speak a word which prepared the way for the future. It was an occasion when one needed to speak out the truth and then wait for a fresh opportunity. Abimelech's reign had to come to an end before Israel would have another chance of good leadership. All Jotham could do was boldly give a prophetic word and then run for his life. But it was a prophetic word that would be fulfilled. Sometimes a situation is so bad all one can do is prepare for the future, and look for God to act.

# Chapter 14

## Injustice Avenged

(Judges 9:22–10:5)

It was a terrible piece of injustice and savagery when Abimelech killed the seventy sons of Gideon who were his half-brothers. We follow the story with an eagerness to know whether God will do anything to honour Gideon who in his early days had been a man of faith?

It often happens in the story of the nations that a terrible injustice is committed. Maybe there is great savagery in the treatment of an enemy, as in the denunciations of Amos against the atrocities of the ancient pagan nations (see Amos 1:3, 6, 9, 11, 13; 2:1). In Abimelech's day the crime was Abimelech's multiple murder of his own half-brothers.

Without repentance, there is no way anything good can come out of Abimelech's murders. All things work together for bad to those who do not love God. God's purpose works against them, not for them. Atrocities are remembered by people and by God.

**Leadership of God's people taken without God's call lacks God's blessing**. Abimelech's stolen rule did not last long (9:22). Eventually the people of Shechem became bitterly disillusioned with the ruler they had chosen for themselves. The ones who were dissatisfied with Gideon's sons become dissatisfied with Abimelech. They acted treacherously in making Abimelech king (see 9:16). Now they act treacherously against Abimelech himself (9:23). Abimelech received back upon himself the very injustice that he had inflicted upon Gideon's sons. An 'evil spirit' arose between Gideon and the people of

Shechem (9:23). 'Evil spirit' here refers to the bitter attitudes that was to be found between Abimelech and the people. We must not read the phrase as if we were reading one of the four gospels.

What happened was entirely within the will of God. God planned that His servant Gideon might be vindicated. Gideon was not perfect but he was God's man for delivering Israel from the Midianites. God had chosen him, despite all of his weaknesses, and God does not like it when one of his chosen instruments is badly used. The 'evil spirit' was from the Lord! God intended that Gideon should be avenged; Abimelech and his relatives would face God's judgement for their murder of Gideon's sons (9:24). Abimelech was told that the greater part of the people of Shechem no longer appreciated his rule. A large number of the men of Shechem became brigands living in the hills, robbing people who passed by and waiting for a chance to attack Abimelech himself (9:25).

**One deception was followed by another**. Gaal rose to power, and the dissatisfied people of Shechem transferred their trust from Abimelech to Gaal (9:26). At the time of a festival, and in the middle of a pagan worship-service (9:27), Gaal asks 'Why should we serve Abimelech and his lieutenant?' (9:28a). He claims things will be different if he becomes ruler of the people (9:30) and arrogantly challenges Abimelech, 'Abimelech, collect your troops and come out and fight!' (9:29b). But he is only pretending to be a valiant warrior. Abimelech is not present, and Gaal is not intending that Abimelech should hear what he says.

Actually Gaal is simply Abimelech all over again. Just as Abimelech enticed the people to himself, so now Gaal entices the people to himself. He dismisses Abimelech's Shechemite ancestry. Abimelech is Gideon's (Baal-Jerub's) son and so he is identified with Gideon. He is building for himself a kingdom, says Gaal, more than he is interested in his mother's Shechemite relatives! The argument subtly undermines Abimelech. The people were deceived by Abimelech; now they are deceived by Gaal. Nothing good can come of the murder of Gideon's sons. When God decides to punish injustice towards His people, all things work together for bad to those who do not love God.

**God's vengeance falls upon the people**. Gaal had not intended that Abimelech should take his challenge seriously, but Zebul, governor of Shechem, is provoked by the humiliating way he had been mentioned (see 9:28). He secretly tells Abimelech what is happening (9:31), and arranges for Abimelech to invade the city abruptly the next day (9:32–33). When God decides to punish sin, things go from bad to worse. And one thing that might rouse God to immediate vengeance is ill-treatment of his people. 'Vengeance is mine; I will repay' says God – and He can act swiftly if His people are badly treated.

Abimelech's soldiers take up concealed positions (9:34). Gaal and Zebul are near the city gate when they invade. 'People are coming down from the tops of the mountains', says Gaal when he sees them from afar. 'No, they are just shadows in the distance', says Zebul. By the time Gaal realizes they are soldiers it is too late to do anything. Zebul has got his revenge. 'Where is your loud-mouthed arrogance now? Go out and fight!' he says to Gaal. Soon Gaal is defeated and removed (9:35–41).

The next day the farmers go out to work in the fields, not realizing that Abimelech (who had once claimed to be related to them) now regarded them as traitors. His soldiers attack again. The people are killed, and the city is destroyed (9:42–45). God's vengeance has come upon all involved in the murder of Gideon's sons.

In 'the tower of Shechem' – apparently a nearby extension of Shechem – the people run to the stronghold of 'El-Berith', a sturdy part of the temple of a pagan god (9:46). They turn to religion! But that does not help them. Abimelech and his men collect wood from a nearby hill and use the wood to turn the fortress into an oven (9:47–49). The people who have taken refuge there perish in the intense heat.

**God's vengeance falls upon Abimelech himself**. Next Abimelech goes to a town to the north of Shechem; it seems that the town had been supportive of Shechem's revolt. He captures the city (9:50). Many citizens take refuge in a tower. One of them drops a millstone on Abimelech and he is mortally injured (9:51–53). With the help of his armour-bearer he prematurely ends his own life (9:54).

It has been a terrible story. All things work together for bad when God decides a time for vengeance has come.

But 'God works all things together for good to those who love him'. There is one way to turn a situation round and that is to seek God in repentance, and put right what can be put right. Only then will God overrule the sins of the past. The past is cleansed by present repentance. Would God do anything to honour Gideon and avenge the murder of his sons? We have our answer. Those who sow seeds of injustice reap a harvest of disaster.

**Disaster was followed by fresh opportunity**. The first few verses of Judges, chapter 10, belong with chapter 9. They let us know that despite the terrible chaos brought into Israel by Abimelech, God still did not abandon them. Tola was raised up to deliver the nation (10:1–2). Jair came a little later (10:3–5). His riding on an ass is a picture of peace and humility. His family's doing the same thing suggests that he mobilized them in the interests of supervising the nation in the ways of peace and prosperity. Abimelech was not the last word in the story of Israel. God avenged the death of Gideon, but His anger does not go on for ever. God gave the nation a fresh chance and sent them two judges to enable the nation to recover. It will be the same for you. Injustice is washed away by extermination, by purifying judgement or by repentance, but whichever way it is God's anger does not continue for ever. The pathway of repentance is best. It takes away God's anger the more speedily.

# *Chapter 15*

# Jephthah's Painful Past

(Judges 10:6–11:11)

Our next judge is Jephthah (10:6–12:7). The same old dreary pattern of sin (10:6), defeat (10:7–9) and distress (10:10) is repeated. God's rescue comes through Jephthah.

1. **God demands that His people spend some time in seeking His rescue**. This time God is slow to rescue them (10:11–14). He points out to them the great ingratitude that they have shown towards Him. God knows how to deal with us wisely. Sometimes He forgives our waywardness very easily. But at other times He knows that we need to be compelled to seek Him. He is not quite so quick about restoring us, and requires that we seek Him. It is not that He needs to delay. The time-gap is not needed by God; it is needed by us His people. Sometimes we need to face the wickedness of our ways and God takes His time about healing and restoring us. So in our story, God's intervention was not quite immediate. He asks them a few questions first.

So the Israelites are brought into deeper repentance before God will help them (10:15–16). They are brought to the point where they are willing for God to do anything, if only He will intervene in their plight. They were in a desperate state. The Ammonites were camped in Gilead ready for war (10:17a); the Israelites were wanting to defend themselves and were looking for a mighty leader (10:17b–18) to make the first blow in the fight.

2. **Israel's saviour was one rejected by his own family but chosen by God**. I could be referring to Jesus! He too was

rejected by his half-brothers but chosen by God. But many of God's men and women of faith follow the same pattern. Jephthah was God's man for the hour! He had a very unhappy family-background. His father was married but at one stage of his life had conceived a son through a girl who was not his wife. The illegitimate son was Jephthah. He was taken into the home and had grown up with the more respectable sons of his father. But his half-brothers despised him (11:1–2). When he was quite young – perhaps in his late teens – Jephthah became the leader of a gang of 'adventurers' (11:3). He was no doubt an unstable and undisciplined character at first, used to doing exactly what he liked, with no one to guide him. He had to cope with the feeling of being rejected by his own family. On the other hand his experience of leadership in his gang of 'adventurers' was good training for the future.

3. **Israel's saviour, rejected by society, is needed by the very people who rejected him**. Some time after Jephthah had been rejected by his own family, the area of Israel around the river Jabbok, called 'Gilead' found itself in trouble (11:4–5). The only person they knew who might help them was Jephthah. So they invited him to be their military leader (11:6).

At first Jephthah protests. 'Did you not throw me out of your very respectable society?' he asks (11:7). They have to humble themselves and admit that the one they rejected is the one they need (11:8). It reminds us of Jesus. The One society rejects is the One they need. Jephthah agrees to help them but he wants to know what his position will be after he has done so. *'Will I really be your head?'* (11:9). This too could be applied to Jesus. When He has rescued us, will He be our ruler? Or do we want His rescue but not His rule? Leadership is a reward. Jephthah looks for recognition. It is something we all want, although some admit it more than others. We like commendation, but it comes as a result of faithfulness.

The people of Gilead agree that Jephthah will be the continuing leader in that part of the land (11:10), and Jephthah agrees to be their leader. He is a young believer. At some stage in his experiences he has come to faith in Yahweh, the God of Israel. They go to Mizpah, a prominent town in the area of Gilead and they publicly proclaim him their leader. Judges 11:11 must mean that Jephthah makes promises before the Lord that he will lead the armies of Gilead with the intent of delivering the people from the Ammonites (11:11).

4. **Israel's saviour has greater gifts than anyone realised**. At this point in the story we get a surprise. Jephthah tries diplomacy before he tries warfare! He sends a message to the Ammonite king asking *'What do you have against us?'* (11:12). He is looking for a way to avert war with the Ammonites. This comes as a bit of a surprise. The men of Gilead did not go to Jephthah because they thought he had gifts of diplomacy. They went to get his help because they thought he would be an ideal leader in war! They were not expecting him to be a peace-maker! Jephthah wanted to go to the negotiating table before he went to the battle field.

Where did Jephthah learn to be a diplomat? What was it that made him look for peace before he went to war? It was undoubtedly something that had arisen in his experience of leading his 'adventurers'. The mob of young men that he had led would have been a unruly and undisciplined gang. There must have been many times when Jephthah had had to settle disputes and keep the peace. Now his past experience comes in useful.

When we are brought into a position of usefulness in God's kingdom we shall find that all of our past experiences make some contribution to where we are now. Our sufferings, our bitter experiences, our loneliness, it will all fit in somewhere, and we shall find that God has been preparing us and training us in readiness for greater ventures for His kingdom. He conceals us in His quiver (see Isaiah 49:2) until He has got us ready as a 'polished arrow' (Isaiah 49:2). A painful past prepares for a present position of usefulness in God's kingdom.

# Chapter 16

## After Peace-Making, Judgement
### (Judges 11:13-28)

The king of the Ammonites has an excuse for his attacks upon Israel. Ammon is demanding territory to be returned which (says the king) was stolen by the Israelites during the time when they first marched into Canaan (11:13). He demands to be given the area to the east of the river Jordan between the Arnon and Jabbok rivers (11:14), the area to the east of the northern half of the Dead Sea.

At this point Jephthah shows a surprising knowledge of Israel's history. He has done his homework and is very familiar with what happened as Israel progressed northwards from the edge of the Sinai desert. Israel did not take any territory belonging to Moab to the south of Ammon; nor did Israel take any of Ammon's territory (11:15). The first territory which Israel met which was related to Abraham and his family was Edom. The Edomites were descended from Esau, Jacob's brother. Israel asked permission to go through their territory but Edom refused (11:16-17a). Then they asked for similar permission from the people of Moab; they were descendants of Lot, Abraham's nephew. Moses was forbidden to attack Edom (see Numbers 20:14-21) or Moab (Deuteronomy 2:9).

So they stopped their northward travels at Kadesh (Judges 11:17b). Later they turned right and went around the territories of Edom (in the south) and Moab (north of Edom) (11:18). When they reached the area north of the Arnon river (Moab's northern boundary) they were coming into an area ruled by Sihon, king of the Amorites. Again Israel asked permission to pass through their territory peaceably (11:19); Sihon refused and attacked Israel (11:20). The war was commenced by Sihon, but the Amorite king was defeated and his territory fell to Israel as a result (11:21–22). No territory of the Ammonites was invaded (note Numbers 20:24).

Jephthah knows all of this and points it out to the Ammonite king. He mentions Moab because some of the territory claimed by the Ammonite king belongs to Moab. Israel captured territory south of Ammon as a result of war. What is interesting in all of this is to note how well Jephthah the 'adventurer', the rejected son of a prostitute, knows the history of the people of God. God made it quite clear that the disputed territory was Israel's (11:23–24). Jephthah says to the king of Ammon 'You take what your god Chemosh gives you!'. He is speaking tactfully and respectfully of the god the Ammonites believe in. Chemosh was actually a Moabite god rather than an Ammonite god. But it seems that the Ammonites conquered Moabite lands north of the river Arnon, and adopted the religion of the area. So 'Chemosh' is the appropriate god to mention when thinking of northern Ammonite territory. The king of the Ammonites would do well to follow the example of Balak king of Moab and keep away from fighting Israel (11:25). Jephthah insists that Israel has occupied the territory of Sihon for a long time; it had never belonged to Ammon. If Ammon attacks Israel God will act as Judge and give victory to Israel (11:26–27).

1. **Some gifted people may be found in some obscure places**. Every part of our story reveals Jephthah as a knowledgeable person, a peaceful person, a diplomat who will turn to war only if he is forced to do so. Who would have thought that Jephthah, the son of a despised harlot, would know so much history! Who would have thought that he could have any political skill at all? But God has a habit of taking ordinary people and – in a way that gives no glory to human cleverness – training them in knowledge and skill ready for usefulness in His kingdom.

God loves to use people whom He has hidden away in

obscure places. Much that God is doing in the world does not get noticed by the rich and the famous. God did not prepare Jesus to be the Saviour in mighty Athens or in Rome or even in Jerusalem. He prepared His Saviour in obscurity.

2. **Jephthah now put his past experience to good use**. He had been used to commanding a band of 'adventurers'. In between his escapades this Jephthah had become a peace-maker, a thinker, a historian, a gifted negotiator. There must have been many times when Jephthah wondered whether anything good would come of his life. All he was good for was leading a mob of rough and tough 'adventurers' who went with him on various mercenary and military escapades. It did not look as if it was the kind of life that would ever do any good for anyone else. But suddenly the very experiences Jephthah had gone through became the very thing that was needed for the people of God. Everything in our past is useful in one way or another. He turned out to have precisely the mixture of experiences that were needed.

3. **Jephthah put peace-making first but was willing to trust God for vindication**. Sadly Jephthah's attempts at peace-making did not do much good (11:28) although it revealed Jephthah as a gifted leader, worthy of a position of leadership in Gilead. Jephthah showed himself a great man when he revealed that he wanted if possible to live at peace with everyone (as Paul might have put it – see Romans 12:18). He was willing to fight as the rest of the story reveals, but conflict was his second choice and peace-making was his first choice.

When he has done his best, he looks to God for help. 'The Lord the Judge be judge this day!' When he has done all that he can to bring about peace, he is ready to take whatever action might be needed and look to God, that God might show in the outcome of events who is right and who is wrong. One day all disputes will be settled. When God acts as Judge, He puts down the wicked and exalts those 'in the right'. He is slow to act as Judge, for He prefers that we find justice in the way of peace. After peace-making comes judgement.

# Chapter 17

## Jephthah's Vow
### (Judges 11:29–40)

Jephthah had to get ready for war. The Spirit of God came upon him (11:29a), and he began to approach the Ammonites (11:29b).

At that point he made a vow. He said to God, *'If you will indeed give the people of Ammon into my power* (11:30), *then it shall happen that whoever shall come out from the doors of my house to meet me, when I return in peace from the people of Ammon, that one shall be for Yahweh, and I shall offer that one up as a burnt offering'* (11:31).

Jephthah was ready to sacrifice a human life as a thank-offering for victory. He leaves it to the providence of God as to who might come from his house first. As a military general he would have a large household of slaves. He did not have a large family. He was not thinking of his much-loved only daughter at the time he made his vow. It is a human being he is thinking of. An 'unclean' animal could not be sacrificed and would not be inside his house. Nor is it likely that he would think of an animal which 'shall come out from the doors of my house to meet' someone. The language speaks of human intention not of a straying animal.

The vow was incredibly foolish and wicked. Jephthah is following the worst war-custom of his day. Human sacrifices were sometimes offered in the ancient world when looking for victory in battle. There was a Moabite king who offered his own son in an attempt to persuade his god to give him victory (see 2 Kings 3:27). It is incredible that Jephthah should have followed this pagan superstition. It shows how true faith and weird superstition can sometimes be found in the same person. (The sacrificing of widows which still takes place in parts of the world today is equally abominable and shows that such weird and evil practises continue in pagan religions.)

1. **Vows often express unbelief or doubt**. Why did Jephthah make this vow? He lacked assurance that God would really hear his prayer for victory. 'If you will really give the people of Ammon into my power . . .'. This way of talking expresses some uncertainty. When we desperately want something we are tempted to start making God promises if only He will hear us. It is good to resolve to show God our gratitude and determine that we shall give back to God something of what God gives to us. Jacob promised to show God gratitude in Genesis 28:20–21. Hannah promised to give her son to the Lord if only she could have a baby boy (1 Samuel 1:11). But we must be careful not to try to bribe God. Many vows are foolish. They lead us into bondage.

I know of a Christian woman who vowed to fast twice a week if God would keep her healthy, but she died from cancer when she was 36 years old. Another friend vowed to fast every Monday. It caused her great agony until the day came when she felt God had released her from foolish legalism. Sometimes a young Christian man vows never to marry, but then falls in love with a sweet attractive Christian lady. Then he does not know what to do about his vow! People make foolish vows about money, about their prayer life, about how obedient they are planning to be. Sometimes people set their sights on having a luxurious life-style, but then calm their conscience by vowing to use their luxurious life for God.

Jesus said 'Swear not at all'. It was a generalisation rather than an absolute law, but as a generalisation it stands! When you feel that God is calling you in a certain direction, don't make a vow about it, just do it! Vows about the future are unnecessary, and bring bondage into our lives. If you feel called to fast once a week, then do it! But don't make a vow about it.

Vows were part of the Mosaic law, but the Christian is not under the law. The are only a few situations where taking a vow is right. Generally speaking 'Swear not at all!'. Jephthah made this foolish vow because he was falling into fear about his success in battle. In his panic he tried to find a way that would persuade God to answer his prayer. But it was needless. God would have answered his prayer without the vow!

2. **God rebuked Jephthah's foolishness**. He went forward to where the Ammonites were, and God gave him victory over them (11:32). Many towns in Ammonite territory were conquered (11:33). It would be many years before the Ammonites could trouble Israel again. Then when Jephthah returns home in triumph. His daughter comes out to meet him (11:34)! God is rebuking Jephthah for his foolish vow. He seems to blame her! *'Oh, my daughter! You have made me miserable and wretched ... !'* It is a weird part of human nature that when we do something ill-advised or foolish we tend to blame the other person. Jephthah does not confess his stupidity in making such a vow. He says 'You have made me miserable' as if it were his daughter's fault (11:35)! But the vow was entirely his doing, not his daughter's. And God was rebuking him for his folly, showing him that He would ridicule any such foolish vow as that. (Something similar happened to Herod Antipas – see Mark 6:22–25.)

3. **Jephthah's foolishness did not stop his being used by God**. One might think that a man who fell into such incredible foolishness as Jephthah did would be left aside by God. But God does not use us because of how sensible we are. He uses us because of His own purpose and graciousness towards us. God rebuked Jephthah's foolishness but He still gave him victory over the Ammonites. What Jephthah achieved, he achieved through faith. What he lost – his own beloved daughter – he lost through doubt and unbelief. But God still used him and he gets a mention in Hebrews 11:32 as a hero of faith.

# Chapter 18

## Faith and Superstition
### (Judges 11:35–40)

It was wicked for Jephthah to make his vow. It was even more wicked for Jephthah to keep it! Evil vows should not be kept; they should be the subject of repentance. The Old Testament law certainly required that vows should be kept. *'I have made a vow ... that I cannot break'*, Jephthah said (11:35) but some vows should be forsaken.

**It is a mistake to confuse faith with superstition**. Jephthah's daughter was like her father, a mixture of devotion and foolishness. Because she was willing to honour her father, she makes no protest but accepts what has happened. She is willing to lose her life rather than have her father break his vow (11:36). She is as godly – and as superstitious – as her father! She asks for time to prepare for her being sacrificed and to say her sad farewells to her friends. They will all be specially sad that she will die without having married and had children (11:37). Jephthah gives her the two months she wants (11:38) and then fulfilled his vow (11:39). At the time when the Book of Judges was written it was still a custom to remember what had happened each year (11:40).

Some have argued that the girl was not really sacrificed but the offering was changed to life-long singleness and work at the tabernacle. I hope they are right! There were situations when the Mosaic law permitted a person to pay money rather than forfeit his life. And we do know that a few years later there were girls who were specially attached to the tabernacle-sanctuary at Shiloh (see 1 Samuel 2:22). It does say 'Jephthah

71

did as he had vowed, and she was a virgin'; it does not say 'Jephthah did as he had vowed, and she died'. So I hope the sacrifice was changed from the death-penalty to something equivalent which allowed Jephthah's daughter her life. But whatever way it was, it was a stupid vow that should have been repudiated with bold faith.

The fact is: faith and superstition often get intertwined. Some people suffer from unbelief. Others suffer from what I can only call over-belief! They get as religious as they can! They get themselves tangled in foolish regulations. They are fearful of enjoying God's world. They fast too much and sleep too little. They ill-treat themselves thinking it is part of their 'religion'. Jephthah was like this. He felt that it needed some kind of religious vow – as extreme as you could get – if God was to answer his prayers. He did not have enough faith in God's amazing grace and goodness. God would have answered their prayers without their foolish religiosity. Such religious regulations 'indeed have an appearance of wisdom', Paul tells us in a similar but different situation (Colossians 2:23). Jephthah's vow is similar to the 'false humility' that Paul referred to.

Of course Jephthah and his daughter were sincere people, godly people. So eager was the daughter to support her father and do what was right, she was willing to lose her prospects of normal married life as an Israelite girl. So willing was her father to be obedient to what he – superstitiously – thought he had to do, that he put aside all natural feeling. He was grief-stricken but (as he saw it) obedient. This is the tragedy about 'zeal without knowledge' (as Romans 10:2 has it). It brings such needless pain.

**Many times we should have the boldness to go higher than the Mosaic law**. 'The law is not of faith'. It is sad that Jephthah's faith could not go higher than the law. It would have been best to disobey the law concerning vows – and even concerning honouring one's father – in faith that this 'disobedience' would be God's will! There are times when we break the law in order to fulfil the law! Legalists like Jephthah do strange things. After the death of Jesus and after Pentecost, the Christian is released from being under the law and is under

Jesus. Jesus fulfilled the Mosaic law for us, and then puts us not under law, but under Himself. Those who walk in the Spirit will fulfil the law accidentally.

If you have made a foolish vow, repent of it! Fall on your knees and ask for mercy. Renounce and repudiate your vow, and never do anything so foolish again. Have faith to go higher than the Mosaic law. If someone else has made a vow on your behalf, it is a time for not honouring your father and mother. You do not honour your father or mother when they sentence you to death! In such a situation the law should be broken!

But 'The law is not of faith' and neither Jephthah or his daughter could rise to such heights. They were not able to think for themselves and sense the leading of the Spirit. David could do it but not Jephthah. When David murdered Uriah the law required David's death. But David ignored the Mosaic law and went directly to God. 'Against **you** ... have I sinned ... Cleanse me with hyssop, and I shall be clean ... You do not delight in sacrifice, or I would bring it ...' (Psalm 51). He was disregarding the Mosaic law and casting himself on God's mercy. By faith he was freeing himself from the judgement of the Mosaic law. David had more boldness of faith than Jephthah.

David had bold faith on more than one occasion. He acted illegally when he helped himself to the consecrated bread at Nob (see 1 Samuel 21:1–6). Ritual law can be broken when necessary. Rahab was guilty of 'false testimony' when she insisted she did not know where the spies were (Joshua 2:4–5).

Trust in Jesus and let His Spirit lead you. Have bold faith. If you make a mistake, get up and move on with God. Don't get into legalistic bondages. Walk under Jesus. Live the life of love. Don't let yourself be led into harshness, severity, and ignorant small-mindedness – all in the name of religion. Jephthah was a good man, but foolishly ignorant. You are not to live like that. You will know the truth in Jesus, and the truth will set you free.

# Chapter 19

## Four Kinds of Personality

(Judges 12:1–15)

Judges chapter 12 brings Jephthah's story to an end (12:1–7) and tells us of three more judges (12:8–15). The four men give us a glimpse of four kinds of leadership, and four kinds of personality.

1. **Jephthah became too much of a tyrant; he was over-concerned with control**. His tyranny began with his resisting a domineering spirit among the Ephraimites (12:1). They were furious that Jephthah, son of a harlot, should have got such a victory against Ammon without consulting the Ephraimites! So they marched northward determined to exterminate Jephthah's family! But Jephthah had become quite domineering himself. There was no way he would yield to them. He reminds them of what they had forgotten. 'I gave you an invitation to join us but at that time you refused. Now you complain. Actually I risked my life in the battle and you were not there to help!' Ephraim started the battle but Jephthah is willing to violently resist Ephraim's ambitious spirit. He gathers his men and commences battle against the Ephraimites (12:4). Then he is determined to carry through the victory to a savage end. Jephthah's men defeat the warriors of Ephraim and then stand guard over the river-crossings ready to catch any Ephraimites seeking to escape back to their home. They have a simple way of finding out who is an Ephraimite. The people of Ephraim used a pronunciation which had no 'sh' sound, and an 'sh' sound is difficult to pronounce if it is not in your mother tongue. The people of

Ephraim could not say a word with 'sh' in it – just as some struggle to say the English 'th'.

Any person crossing the river was asked to say 'shibboleth'. If he could not say it but said 'sibboleth' instead, they knew he was an Ephraimite (12:5–6). In this way forty-two thousand Ephraimites were caught and killed.

The story of Jephthah ends with a note that he ruled for six years and was honourably buried in Gilead (12:7). But the story of Jephthah does not have a happy ending. He did not like the domineering spirit of the Ephraimites, but he himself went much too far in punishing them and wiping them out of existence as much as he could. The truth was he had a domineering spirit himself at this point. He could not bear a rival, certainly not one who wished to domineer, and took his determination to be free of anyone's control much too far. He was an autocrat determined to exterminate other autocrats.

2. **Ibzan was a multi-tribalist; he was concerned with national unity**. He was convinced that multi-tribal marriage was the answer to Israel's needs (12:8–10). He got his own family to practise inter-clan marriage. It was a way of trying to get Israel to be a united country rather than one divided up by tribal interests. Those of us who live in Africa can learn something from it! But there are other forms of 'tribalism'. Many countries have factional disputes. There is the rich clan and the poor clan, the university clan and the not-so-educated clan who despise the posh accent. Tribalism takes many forms.

Ibzan saw the problem and resolved to do what he could about it. He persuaded his family to forget the idea of staying within their own clan, and encouraged them to develop wider interests and even to get married 'outside the clan'. Small-minded parochialism is dangerous for a leader, dangerous for a country, and dangerous for the church of Jesus Christ. For God might be working powerfully in another circle of Christians other than our own – in another clan we might say.

3. **Elon was a traditionalist; he was concerned with keeping things as they had been for a long time**. Elon is known only for living, dying and getting buried! The two verses of Judges

12:11–12 tell us nothing more. One wonders why a leader of Israel should be mentioned at all if he was only known for living, dying and getting buried. He was a leader of Israel so the writer felt he had to be mentioned. Yet nothing of his story is told, presumably because there was not much to tell. There are some people whose temperament is such that they just want to keep things going as they are. Their weakness is passivity. When their life is all over, they have lived, they have had a title as 'leader' but nothing much has changed. They get an honourable burial, but no one ever looks back to them as having achieved very much.

4. **Abdon was a communicator; he was concerned to keep everyone well informed throughout the land**. Abdon was famous for having sons and grandsons who rode on donkeys (12:13–15). This is not so odd as it might seem. He mobilized his family to travel around the land. People everywhere would get to see his sons and his grandsons travelling around on donkeys. It was not that he and his family were eager to be powerful and rich. Horses were known for being expensive and for being used for warfare and battle (see Joshua 11:4 and elsewhere). But asses or donkeys were cheaper. Horses were used for war. Asses and donkeys were used for travel and communication. The picture is one of a family who got around, travelled far and wide in their community and found out what was going on.

So the four men introduce us to four types of personality, four styles of leadership. One became a dictator; one was the very opposite passively letting circumstances dictate to him. two of them were much wiser watching over the unity of the nation and keeping themselves well-informed.

A Christian inevitably compares all four men to Jesus, the greatest leader and the Head of the people of God ruling from the right-hand of the Father. He is firm but not dictatorial. He likes us to 'wish' to follow Him. He is taking His church to where He wants it to go. He is not happy just to 'keep the wheels turning'. Above all He wants His people to be one, knowing each other, well-informed about each other, one body, one holy nation under Jesus.

# Chapter 20

## Manoah and His Wife

(Judges 13:1–23)

Once again Israel follow the wretched pattern of sin and defeat (13:1). The judge God sends them eventually is Samson.

A Danite couple cannot have children (13:2). One day 'the angel of the Lord appears' to the wife (13:3). It is an appearance of God Himself, although Manoah's wife is not seeing the 'stuff' – the innermost essence – of God. She is seeing a **representation** of God. No one can see God and live (John 1:18) but God can use angels to make something visible that represents Him. Manoah's wife is to have a child who will be a Nazirite all his life and even before he is born! Manoah's wife is to avoid wine and ceremonially 'unclean' food (that is, declared unclean by the Mosaic law) so that the boy is a Nazirite even in the womb (13:4)! When the son is born his uniqueness and sacredness to God will be marked by his never having his hair cut. He has a very special destiny: to start the process of delivering Israel from the Philistines (13:5). It would not be finished until the days of David, but Samson's destiny was to start the battle for freedom from the Philistines.

Each time the Israelites fall into sin, the depth of their fall is deeper than before. Now their defeat by the Philistines is very serious and it will be generations before they are released from Philistine domination.

1. **Manoah and his wife are treated differently by the angel**. The angel appears only to Manoah's wife, not to Manoah

himself. Only Manoah's wife is told of the birth. Only she is given instructions. Only she is told of the destiny of the child. Perhaps the reason for this is that it is Manoah's wife who specially has to avoid wine and unclean food, but it seems strange that Manoah himself is not at first involved. Manoah's wife tells her husband what has happened but he knows of it only through her (13:6–7).

Why should God treat Manoah and his wife differently. One can think of several reasons. God is sovereign and likes to treat each person individually. Husbands and wives each have to have their own distinct relationship with God. Each person is a distinct personality, with different temperaments. The fact that one person gets visions and dreams and another person gets revelations in an entirely different way – perhaps less dramatically – need not worry any of us. We have different needs, different personalities, and God treats us according to His own will and our own needs.

The fact that God treats each person individually tests us. It determines whether we have problems with jealousy or with pride. Manoah is in danger of jealousy. Why should his wife get visited by an angel but he be left out? Manoah's wife is in danger of spiritual pride. She might say to herself 'I have been visited by an angel, but my husband has not! Perhaps I am spiritually superior to my husband'.

2. **Manoah and his wife respond well to their different spiritual experiences**. I said that they were both **in danger** of reacting badly, but actually they both react rather well. Manoah does the right thing. If you are left behind in some spiritual experience, the best thing to do is pray, and that is what Manoah does, asking that he might be told about the boy for himself. He says *'Please let the man of God ... come to us again ...'* (13:8). He does not want to leave out his wife – he does not say 'come to **me**' – but he wants to be included in what has happened to his wife.

The result is surprising. The text says 'God listened to the voice of **Manoah**; and the angel of God came again to the **woman** ...' (13:9)! Manoah's prayer is heard but he is still left out of the experience of the angelic visitation! Once again there is a test: will one of them respond with jealousy or pride?

Manoah's wife does the right thing also. Just as Manoah prayed 'Please let the man of God ... come to **us** again ... ', so Manoah's wife did not want Manoah to be left out of the angelic visitation. She made the angel wait while she ran quickly to get her husband (13:10)! Neither Manoah nor his wife wanted the other spouse to be left out of what was happening. Although God was treating them individually, they were each wanting to move together without the other partner being left behind. It is a sweet and tender picture of a couple where neither wanted to be left out of what was happening to the other. Husbands and wives could learn a lot from it! (One could compare this story with the story of Abraham and Sarah where Sarah seems to have been left out of what was happening to Abraham, and the incident with Hagar was the result! Abraham has a revelation that a child was to be born from his own body, Genesis 15:4. It led Sarah into a mistake – Genesis 16:2. God had a revelation which included Sarah but it came to Abraham not to her – see Genesis 18:10.)

3. **Manoah's wife is ahead of her husband in using spiritual logic**. The couple catch up with each other and they receive the message from the angel together (13:11–14). They are hospitable to the angel and as a result discover that they have been speaking to the angel of the Lord (13:15–21), whose name and nature can never be fully revealed (13:15–21). This alarms Manoah. *'We shall surely die ... ',* he says (13:22). At this point the woman uses what we can call spiritual logic. *'If the Lord had desired to kill us, He would not have ... shown us all these things ... '* (13:23). Spirituality involves making some deductions from the goodness of God; some more examples are found in Matthew 6:25–30; Romans 5:10; 8:31–35. So Manoah's wife helps her husband to see that all will be well. God is working in their lives. He has no plans to kill them, only plans to bless them.

# Chapter 21

## Samson at Timnah

(Judges 13:24–14:19)

There are really only two stories about Samson: (i) the story of his marriage to a Philistine woman and the various events that resulted from it (14:1–15:20). It ends by noting how Samson came to lead Israel for twenty years (15:20). Then (ii) there is the story of the events that led up to Samson's great victory at the time of his death (16:1–31). The repetition of Judges 15:20 in Judges 16:31 highlights the division of the stories into two sections.

As the angel promised, the child was born. He was named 'Samson' ('Sunny'). He came to faith in the God of Israel. On one occasion when he was at a place called 'Mahaneh Dan', the Spirit of God began arousing him and empowering him for his particular ministry (13:24–25).

The story comes swiftly to the opening event in Samson's conflict with the Philistines. He falls in love with a Philistine woman in Timnah. Although the Israelites and Philistines were hostile towards each other they occupied the same territory. Samson had great strength of body and great strength of personality. He was naturally overbearing, domineering, masterful. He was self-willed, arrogant, and always was strongly drawn to a good-looking woman. When he sees a fascinating, good-looking woman, the woman of Timnah, he decides he must have her as his wife (14:1–2), and that she will be his way of getting into the society of the Philistines. The protest of his parents could not change his mind (14:3). There was no law against marrying a Philistine, although most Israelite parents would not have thought it a good idea.

Judges 14:4 says 'His father and mother did not know that this was from Yahweh, for *'he sought an opportunity against the Philistines.'* But who is this 'he'? Does it refer to God? Or does it refer to Samson? A study of Judges shows, I believe, that it refers to Samson. It comes clear that Samson was seeking an opportunity against the Philistines. He was mixing business and pleasure in befriending the woman of Timnah!

God was determined to use Samson. The birth-story of Judges 13 makes it clear that God had made Samson the way that he was! Even his weaknesses of character would be used by God. Like left-handed Ehud, God would use His servant Samson just as he was – and indeed God had made him the way that he was. Whatever failings Samson may have had, he was a man of faith with a determination to put down the power of the Philistines.

**Samson is a classic case of God's working through a person's own personality and desires**. Samson 'was seeking an occasion to confront the Philistines'. One might ask, did God need Samson to 'seek an occasion' to deal with the Philistines. Why did He not just pour out fire and sulphur upon them from heaven as He did upon Sodom and Gomorrah? Why did He not just send Samson and give him a miraculous victory, in the way that He sent Gideon and gave him a miraculous victory?

God works at different ways at different times. (i) Sometimes He works by sheer miracle, without human agency. No human being was involved in pouring out fire and sulphur upon Sodom. (ii) Sometimes He works through miracles which make use of human obedience. Gideon's defeat of Midian was miraculous but it involved Gideon's obedience. (iii) Sometimes God works through human character, empowered by the Holy Spirit. This third option was the way God worked through Samson. He used Samson himself. God gave Samson himself unusual power and strength that came through the anointings of the Spirit. Samson was not a very religious man, but God was using him anyway! Samson had his own wishes and desires, and God was working through them. Samson was a man of faith, but his style of living had a certain shape to it that depended on the kind of person that Samson was.

Samson and his parents go down to Timnah to prepare for a marriage. On the way Samson wanders off alone into the vineyards of Timnah and kills a lion with his bare hands, but his parents did not know about that incident (14:5–6). They meet the woman (14:7) and the marriage is arranged.

Later they go down again for the wedding. By this time, some bees have made a nest in the carcass of the lion and Samson gets some honey for himself and his parents. Still the parents do not know about the killing of the lion (14:8–9).

The wedding feast would be seven days long. The father sees the woman to arrange the marriage (10:10). The bride's family provide thirty men to be friends and companions to Samson (10:11). Then Samson arranges a kind of contest with his thirty bridegrooms. They are asked to decipher a riddle, as a form of entertainment during the wedding. There was a lot of money involved, because thirty suits of clothing would be valuable (10:12–13a). The thirty men accept the challenge (14:13b), but actually Samson's riddle is exceptionally difficult. Samson has played a trick on them. There is no way they will be able to guess what it means. 'Out of the eater something to eat; out of the strong, something sweet' (14:14). What can it mean?

For three days they puzzle over it. On the fourth day they use Samson's intended wife to get the secret, threatening her with death if she does not co-operate (14:15). For the rest of the seven days (which is what verse 17 means) she uses her tears and nagging to get the secret out of him and then tells the thirty Philistine companions of Samson (14:16–17). They answer the riddle (14:18a) but Samson knows how they got the answer (14:18b). Then comes a dramatic turn. Samson is furious, but the Spirit of God comes down upon him. There is a mixture of human anger and divine enablement. He goes down to Ashkelon, more than twenty miles away, robs thirty Philistines of their clothes and pays his debt to the thirty companions (14:19a). God's plan and Samson's own character have worked together to strike the first blow in the harassing of the Philistines.

# Chapter 22

## Being Oneself

(Judges 14:19–15:17)

Samson was angry with his wife and went back to his father's house without her (14:19b). The woman's father thinks the marriage is finished but does not want his daughter to be abandoned in disgrace. He persuades Samson's friend to take her on as his wife (14:20). Presumably he was a young man looking for a wife.

Samson was used by God along the lines of his own character. There was one disadvantage in this. **When you are used by God along the lines of your own worldly, human, self-centred character, it does not bring much blessing for you yourself personally**. Samson was used by God but did not get much spiritual joy for himself. His relationship with the woman was not close. She nagged him but did not trust him enough to share with him what was happening. When you are a rough careless character you might be used by God despite yourself. Yet you do not get much of the personal fellowship that comes from God Himself. Even Balaam's ass was used by God. God can use anyone, even a donkey. But the deepest pleasures of life, such as close intimacy with a good companion, the presence of God in one's life – these things do not come just by being a tool in God's hands. The deepest blessings of life require some changes in our own character. The greatest privileges come through honouring God at a deeper level. Samson was a man of faith but he was missing the deepest pleasures of life because God was using him despite his wildness. There is no mention of prayer or revelations from God in this part of the story. A more spiritual lifestyle would have led Samson into a knowledge of God at a deeper level. But this was missed by Samson altogether.

Some time after Samson's marriage he goes back to Timnah to get reconciled to his wife. It is May, wheat-harvest time, a sunny, dry, time of the year. When he arrives he finds that his father-in-law is embarrassed. The poor start to Samson's married life made the father think Samson had abandoned his wife. The girl had been married off to someone else (15:1–3)!

Once again the incident is used in Samson's life to rouse him to intimidate and terrorize the Philistines. He determines to get revenge (15:4). His being offended was typical of his entire story. He is offended both as an individual and as a judge; the two aspects of his life are intertwined. God wants someone who explodes likes a volcano when the Philistines are around! And he had just the man he wanted in Samson! But it is more than that. **God produced Samson!** He superintended the birth of Samson in the womb – which is the point of the story of Judges 13. God did not look around and find the best that He could get when He found Samson; He made Samson the way that he was! He needed someone exactly as Samson was!

So Samson went and caught three hundred foxes and tied all their tails together with rope (15:4). Then he put 'torches' on the ropes. I suppose he got pieces of cloth, dipped them in oil, and then set the oily rags on fire. Then he let loose the foxes. We have already been told it was a dry time of the year. The foxes ran all over the place, pulling this way and that, and the burning torches set the fields of wheat on fire. The entire Philistine grain harvest was ruined. It was a clever trick. Only 'sunny boy Samson' could have done it!

The Philistines soon found out what had led to the burning of their fields. Instead of attacking Samson – who was a rather intimidating figure to attack – they got their revenge on the woman of Timnah and her father (15:6). That made Samson even more angry. He welcomed every opportunity to attack the Philistines; that was his calling in life. He attacked them and smote them 'high on the hip' (as the Hebrew has it; it is a popular expression meaning 'ruthlessly'). With enormous physical strength he slaughtered vast numbers of Philistines (15:7–8a).

Once again we notice how Samson's character and his calling flowed together in partnership. When Samson slaughtered these Philistines he was fulfilling his calling, but at the same time he was being himself!

In all of this **Samson is a classic case of salvation by the grace of God**. Of course, every believer is saved by grace – but this is more visible in some cases than in others. When nice people are saved, we tend to think they are saved by their niceness! But Samson was a spoilt, self-centred man, whose way of serving God was very much tied into his own character. He was on three occasions powerfully but foolishly drawn to a good-looking woman. He rebelled against being a Nazirite. But God used all of this. We had best believe Samson was 'saved by grace'. He certainly could not have been saved in any other way.

Samson's slaughtering of the Philistines made them thirsty for revenge. Samson withdrew to a well-known cave (15:9b) and an army of Philistine soldiers came looking for him (15:10). The people of Judah – three thousand of them – have no choice but to hand Samson over to them, but he agrees to be taken captive easily by his own people (15:11–13). He is sent unarmed and bound with ropes towards the Philistines at a place called Lehi (15:14). Seeing him apparently helpless they rush towards him in great glee expecting to easily kill him (15:15). Then – as Samson knew would happen – he is given miraculous power by the Spirit. He breaks free from the ropes which tie him. He picks up the jaw-bone of an ass lying nearby and, using it as a weapon, slaughters a thousand Philistines before the rest flee in terror (15:16–17). **Just by being himself**, Samson has won a great victory for God.

# Chapter 23

## Learning to Pray
(Judges 15:18–20)

A little incident after the slaughter at Lehi is one of the
greatest turning points in Samson's life. He had slaughtered a
thousand men single-handedly. But it left him totally dehy-
drated and utterly weak. At that point any Philistine could
easily have killed him – and there were some Philistines
around after the slaughter of their companions who would
have been delighted to despatch Samson from this world
altogether. For the first time in the story of Samson, he prays!
I suppose he had prayed before, but you would hardly know
it from the story of Judges 14:1–15:17. Prayer is totally
unmentioned. It does not seem to have been a great priority
in Samson's life until now.

But now Samson is desperate. God had given Samson a gift
of physical strength but now, just after many Philistines have
just been mightily defeated, the gift of physical strength is not
functioning and any passing Philistine would have been able
to defeat Samson!

There is nothing he could do except pray! He gives thanks
for the recent victory, and he pleads the desperation of his
plight (15:18).

God works a miracle for him! A miniature earthquake takes
place and a spring opens up from the ground right near to
Samson. Fresh water gushes forth from the new spring.
Samson quenches his terrible thirst and his strength returns
to him (15:19).

Judges 15:20 closes this part of the story. The recent events of intimidating the Philistines and curtailing their activities had proved to everyone that Samson was a worthy leader for the nation, despite his rough and wild ways. He led Israel for twenty years during the days of the Philistines, preventing their power from getting worse, and fulfilling the call that had been predicted for him (see 13:5).

1. **He accepted the call imposed upon him**. God's call to Samson came before he was born. He was a Nazirite, one specially dedicated to God, even in his mother's womb. Samson's call was not a casual invitation; it was an authoritative demand. God gave him very little choice. It is wonderful when we have a clear calling from God and we know what it is. 'Woe to me if I do not preach the gospel', said the apostle Paul. He knew clearly what his calling from God was; he had very little choice in the matter.

2. **His sense of calling enabled Samson to move with assured faith**. For most of his life he is gripped with the conviction that God will work for him. When he killed the lion at the time of his visit to Timnah, he kept quiet about it. He knew that it would be used by God in some way in provoking the Philistines and opening up the way for their downfall. When he allowed the people of Judah to send him bound and apparently helpless to the waiting Philistines he knew that God's Spirit would empower him. Later in the Bible Samson is known as a hero of faith (see Hebrews 11:32). He constantly lived with great assurance. Until Judges 15:18 there never is the slightest feeling in the story of Samson that he had any doubts about himself or about his way of doing God's will. When questioned by his parents he calmly overruled them and insisted on his own way. He knew God's will! His parents did not know what was happening but he did.

3. **He was slow to attend to his own character**. God's will and Samson's will were constantly intertwined. God used his violent and vindictive nature, his determination to avenge the wrongs committed by the Philistines. But this is a difficult way to live. It will get him into trouble eventually. When one gets one's own way too much, when everything one does for God easily agrees with what one wants to do anyway,

there is a danger that the sinfulness of our own nature is not attended to.

4. **Samson came to a crisis when his physical strength failed him**. His exhaustion after the slaughter at Lehi let him know – if he did not know it before – that without God's special help he could be vulnerable to easy defeat. He could not rely on his gift; he had to learn to rely on God. His gift of strength could let him down, and almost did let him down at Lehi.

There is something prophetic and parabolic about the miraculous quenching of Samson's thirst. He knew he was desperately thirsty. He told God of his desperate need. God dramatically opened up a supply of living water for him. The supply was not enough; he needed to drink from it, Steady drinking produced steady recovery. It was a lesson he never forgot. The place became known as 'The well of the one who calls'. From that time forward his gifting and his knowledge of God led into a lifetime of ministry towards the people of God.

Each aspect of the matter expresses principles that Samson perhaps would remember and we would do well to apply to ourselves. We too, in our own way, know what it is to be thirsty. Jesus gave an invitation: 'If any person thirsts...'. Jesus too promised that a supply of living water would be opened to us. We too have to find out the secret of drinking from Jesus, God's well of living water. The mighty Samson could become a weakling. The one who has slaughtered a thousand could himself be slaughtered by any passing Philistine. He needed to live not upon his gift, but upon the moment-by-moment powerful activities of God. We ourselves have to learn similar lessons. We too have to learn to be strong in the Lord and in His mighty power. 'Out of his innermost being flows rivers of living water.' This Jesus said of the Spirit which those who believe should receive.

# Chapter 24

## Samson and Delilah

(Judges 16:1–21)

The story moves forward about twenty years, from the beginning of Samson's ministry to the end of his ministry, from how his judgeship began to how his judgeship ended.

1. **Samson uses a risky method of provoking the Philistines**. He goes to Gath, the southernmost Philistine town. There must have been some plan in his mind involving the Philistines. He deliberately chose a Philistine town a long way from his home. Yet he must have known that his visit could not be kept secret. There was only one way into the town – through the town gates. Samson surely knew that it would hardly be possible for such a famous person as he was to enter the town unnoticed. Ancient towns were only small villages. Strangers could not enter them without being noticed. One remembers also Samson's long hair which must have made him conspicuous. It seems he was looking out for a way to provoke the Philistines once again and was walking deliberately into a dangerous situation – something he had done before. *'He saw there a prostitute'* (16:1). Once again Samson decides to use a woman as a means of provoking the Philistines.

Judges 16 begins in the same way as Judges 14–15. In both cases he makes use of a woman to provoke the Philistines (14:1; 16:1). Yet there is a deterioration between the events of Judges 14–15 and the events of Judges 16 twenty years later. The woman of Timnah he wanted for his wife. The girl in Gaza he wanted for a few hours. Judges 14–15 contain references to the Spirit's leading Samson, but chapter 16 contains no reference to the Holy Spirit.

The citizen's discover Samson's presence (16:2). Of course! Samson must have known it would happen, and must have planned for it to happen. He was mixing business and pleasure again! The Philistines are nervous about apprehending Samson – he had been known to kill a thousand of them without help! They decided to ambush him at the town gate. When he passes through the gate in the morning he will – they think – have been awake much of the night with his new acquaintance. They plan to capture him then when he is tired and unprepared. They wait 'in' the city gate, that is, in the rooms by the side of the gate itself.

But Samson knows that they will be trying to capture him. He leaves the girl earlier than anyone would imagine, sets off home, and deliberately does something provocative that will vex the Philistines and provoke them into a fight. He walks off with large parts of the gate and dumps them on the top of a hill in Hebron, 40 miles away, in the heart of Judah (16:3)! Samson's purpose seems to have been to deliberately provoke the Philistines. He is once again, wanting to set in motion a train of events in which he will harass and trouble the Philistines.

Samson's habit of mixing business and pleasure was dangerous. Admittedly, there was more to what he was doing than simply spending a night with an immoral girl. He would not have needed to go to Gaza for that! Samson deliberately chose a Philistine town to visit and deliberately enraged the Philistines against himself in a way that did not drag the whole of Israel into a war they would not be able to win.

2. **Samson allowed himself to be pressed into unfaithfulness to God**. Before anything more could develop in the relationships between Samson and the Philistines, something happened which brought about a new turn of events. He fell in love with Delilah! He had always had an eye for a good-looking woman. He had always liked to mix business and pleasure and involve an attractive woman in his schemes against the Philistines. It always had dangers attached to it and now Samson gets into bad trouble. Delilah came from the valley of

Sorek (16:4), a deep valley about ten miles west of Jerusalem. She probably was an Israelite woman since her name is a Hebrew name. But she is more interested in how she can exploit Samson's love for her than she is in Samson himself. Samson is in love with her; she is only in love with what she can get out of him. The leaders of the five Philistine towns know how difficult it is to capture Samson and each offer her eleven hundred pieces of silver – a total of five thousand five hundred – if she can find a way of their being able to immobilize him (16:5). Samson unbound would be too dangerous a prisoner.

Delilah tries to find out his secret. 'Please tell me where your great strength is . . . ', she asks (16:6; see also 16:10, 13a). He gives three answers (16:7, 11, 13b) and each time she tests his answer (16:8, 12a, 14a) and finds out that he has not told her the truth. Each time she wakes him up suddenly (16:9a, 12b, 14b), but three times he shows that he still has his strength (16:9b, 12c, 14c). She pretends it is a kind of playful game but each time she has Philistines nearby ready to capture Samson if he should be telling the truth (14:9, 12).

Samson maintains his secret. He knows that he has been chosen from birth for the work of beginning to deliver Israel from the Philistines (see 13:5), and he knows that his 'Naziriteship' – his special selection for his work – is signified by his never having his hair cut with a razor (see 13:5). His uncut hair is a sign of his calling and a sign of God's unfailing faithfulness to him. When his hair is cut off, his special strength as a Nazirite will be cut off also.

Eventually Samson allows himself to be pressed into unfaithfulness to God (16:15–21). Soon he betrays his secret, displeases God and ruins his life. It is not that Samson himself had his hair shaved. It was done to him while he was entirely passive, while he was asleep. But his bad company had led him into something he never intended.

# Chapter 25

## Samson Persists in Faith
(Judges 16:15–31)

3. **Samson allowed himself to become gullible**. Samson had
twice used a woman to find a way to provoke the Philistines.
His brief marriage to the woman of Timnah was (among other
things) his chosen way of getting into the society of the
Philistines. He went to the girl at Gaza, intending to use her
to provoke the Philistines. He had twice 'mixed business with
pleasure' and used a girl to fulfil his own purposes. But now
there is a girl who is also mixing business (five thousands
pieces of silver and more) with pleasure (having Samson as a
lover). This time it is not Samson using the girl; it is the girl
using Samson. She has no real love for Samson. All along she
is working only for her silver. She pretends she wants an
assurance of his love (16:15) and nags him daily, pestering him
until he tells her what she wants to know (16:16). There is not
the slightest love or sincerity in her; she only wants the reward
of silver. Samson had become gullible. Before he had his own
schemes when he used the two women in his life. Now this
third woman in his life has her schemes to use him. He has
become susceptible to trickery. True love is wide awake;
Samson's kind of love for Delilah made him vulnerable to
Delilah's counterfeit affection.

Previously, Samson had his own schemes when he used the
two women in his life. Now the third woman in his life has her
schemes to use him. He believes her utterly but he has become
naive. How trustworthy is a woman who loves money too
much? Samson is open to deception. He reveals what he

should not reveal (16:17). She has no love for him and is quite willing to hand him over to the brutality and vindictiveness of the Philistines. She gets her money (16:18), arranges for the shaving of Samson's head (16:19), and – just in case he should be deceiving her again! – playfully calls for the Philistines (16:20a).

By letting the sign of his call be removed Samson grieved the Holy Spirit without even knowing about it. He learned from painful experience that God had left him to his own strength and that his miraculous gift of strength had been withdrawn (16:20b). His enemies soon began to torment him (16:21).

In the New Testament Samson is portrayed as a hero of faith (Hebrews 11:32). Despite his wild ways he was a man who believed God, and believed that he would fulfil his calling. He came to the greatest height of faith in the last days of his life. He had ruined his life. God had left him. His strength was withdrawn. The sign of his being a Nazirite had been removed. Yet it is at this point that Samson shows the greatest faith he ever had. He still believed God could use him! Despite all that had happened to him and the tragedy of his betrayal by Delilah he was still trusting God and looking for God to work on his behalf.

4. **Samson gained victory amidst defeat**. His hair was growing again (16:22)! Why should not restored hair mean restored Naziriteship? Samson was still a man of faith. He had trusted God many times before. God had always given him strength when he needed it. Did he really have to believe that he was finished for ever and that God would never use him again. No, he believed the opposite. He believed that God could restore him and that he could be used by God again.

The day came when the Philistines were thoroughly enjoying their victory over Samson. The various rulers of the Philistine towns came together to celebrate their victory and give praise to their god, Dagon (16:23). They give the honour for their victory to Dagon (16:24). They want to gloat over Samson's defeat and get him to entertain them while he is in his chains. They put him near the pillars holding up the temple (16:25).

But Samson is still a man of faith despite all that has happened to him. He is blind but he still has an idea for defeating the Philistines, and he has an instinctive faith that God will hear him. He asks to be placed closer to the pillars holding up the temple so that he can feel them (16:26). There are thousands of Philistines present with their leaders (16:27). Samson still believes God is with him. He continues to be a man of faith despite his failures and mistakes. He still is praying, still wants to mix his own wishes (vengeance) with the needs of God's kingdom (defeat of the Philistines). He pulls the two columns between which he is standing and – accepting that his death will be the price of victory – pulls the building down (16:28–30a). It was his greatest triumph ever against the Philistines. For many years their power to harass the Israelites would be severely reduced. He had fulfilled his life's calling! God had said 'he shall begin to deliver Israel from the hands of the Philistines' (13:5) and Samson had achieved God's purpose for his life. His dying moments achieved more than his entire previous life (16:30b). He received an honourable burial (16:31) and went down in history as one of the men of faith who had contributed to the progress of God's kingdom.

Samson had weaknesses of character. His overbearing, self-willed, arrogant ways might make us think he was unsuited to the kingdom of God. His powerful sexuality might seem to be one of his weak points. But when the story is all over we can see that God used Samson as he really was. Samson achieved something for the kingdom of God while being just the sort of person he was by nature. One thing was in his favour. He believed God again and again, even to the very end. And a man who goes on believing God will in the end achieve something for God.

# Chapter 26

## Idolatrous Chaos
### (Judges 17:1–18:5)

Our story of twelve judges has come to an end. The question now is: what is the state of Israel now that the twelve judges have finished their work? The answer is: worse than ever! When each judge died, the people returned to ways that were even more corrupt than those of the previous generation (see Judges 2:19). The overall situation was declining despite periodic rescues and revivals.

1. **Drifting from God leads a society into chaotic ignorance**. An Ephraimite called Micah stole eleven hundred shekels of silver from his mother. Not knowing who had taken her money, the mother cursed whoever the thief might be. Micah was present at the time of her curse, and was so distressed at being cursed by his mother that he confessed to what he had done. The mother's curse was replaced by a mother's blessing (17:1–2).

The mother let Micah have two-elevenths of the money. She wanted him to have enough money to make an 'image and idol' (two words for one object) which was meant to represent Yahweh, the God of Israel (17:3–4). The new idol was placed in a shrine which Micah already used for worship. The shrine already had an ephod (some kind of container with stones in it which were used like dice for discovering God's will) and it had some additional idols. One of Micah's sons became a priest in the sanctuary (17:5).

All of this was idolatrous. Yahweh was not meant to be worshipped via images. All priests were meant to be members of the tribe of Levi. And a man who robs his mother and then becomes religious is a strange kind of worshipper! *'In those days Israel had no king . . . '* (17:6).

The scene changes. One day a Levite left Bethlehem looking for a job (17:7). He happened to pass Micah's home (17:7) and Micah thought he was just the man he wanted to be the priest in his sanctuary (17:8–9). So the Levite was given the job that previously had been done by one of Micah's sons (17:10–12). It made Micah feel sure that God would prosper him (17:13).

Almost everything in this story is wrong. One should not rob mothers. One should not curse thieves. One should not make images of Yahweh. One should not keep private sanctuaries for idols. You should not consecrate a priest if you are not yourself a high-priest. Only a Levite descended from Aaron and appointed in Jerusalem by the high-priest can be any true priest in Israel. But a Levite should not have to go looking for a job. A Levite who is not descended from Aaron should not be a priest at all. This entire story is a string of events that ought not to have happened!

The problem was – as the narrator points out – that there was no king in Israel. King David, who came later, would never allow such idolatrous nonsense to exist in Israel.

The story is a picture of everyone 'doing what is right in his own eyes'. It is not (be it noticed) a matter of doing what is wrong, but of doing what is **right** – in one's own eyes. No one felt they were doing anything wrong! The people actually felt good about what they were doing. The mother thought it right to curse a thief. Micah thought it right to build a shrine for his gods. They both thought it was a good idea to add another god, an idol representing Yahweh. They thought a priest for the idol would be a good idea, and a Levite was the best man for the job. Worst of all – in abysmal ignorance – Micah thought Yahweh would prosper him for his weird religion.

Before we denounce Micah too much we ought to remember times when we have done similar things. How ignorant of God we all are by nature! It needs a miracle of grace before any of us see things as they really are. How superstitious we get. What incredible stupidities there are in many modern religions! How cruel religious people can be. Robbing a mother of her silver and then going to the sanctuary – to prop up the little idols! But we have often been equally stupid.

The story is one of grotesque and hideous ignorance. What sort of religion is it that encourages a man to rob his mother? He is so superstitious that his mother's curse terrifies him. He claims to be an Israelite yet does not even obey the Ten Commandments. Has he never heard of 'You shall not make for yourself a graven image...'? Apparently not. The story lets us see that drifting from God leads a society into chaotic ignorance.

Next comes a third stage in the story (after two in 17:1–6, 7–13). The tribe of Dan had never obtained its 'inheritance' in the land of Israel. They had been allocated their territory but had never taken it (compare Joshua 19:40–46 and Judges 1:34). Now they decide to look for an inheritance elsewhere (18:1). They send out five men representing the tribe (18:2a). They come to the hill-country of Ephraim. As they are passing Micah's house they hear the voice of the Levite priest. Maybe he is loudly reciting some prayers for the family. His accent is not Ephraimite and they are curious to find out whose voice it is. They discover the shrine and ask the Levite how he came to be there (18:3). Soon they are asking for an oracle to let them know whether their expedition will be successful (18:4–5). Yes, says the Levite, God approves your venture. Go in peace.

It is all a terrible description of dead, decayed, disastrous religion. The people of Israel had deteriorated to a level of chaotic idolatry with all of its accompanying religiosity. This is what religious decline is like. When there is no God-given leader the state of a nation or of a church will decline. The result is chaotic ignorance. Mothers are ill-treated. Cursing abounds. People remain religious but their religion is weird and ignorant. Being a priest becomes a profession and such professionals go around looking for a job. They are consulted by people who want to satisfy their inclination to have God on their side. Those who want to earn money by giving religious oracles make sure that they give ones that encourage the enquirer and keep him coming (plus the right fee) for more assurance that their expeditions will be successful. 'Go in peace', the religious professionals say. But it is not going in peace; it is going around in appalling superstition and religious delusion.

The point of the story is to show us the desperate need for a king in Israel. Only God's king would receive a revelation of what God wanted. Only God's king would reveal a holy God. Only God's king would provide true salvation. David was His prototype; Jesus would be the fulfilment of the royal pattern that He initiated.

# Chapter 27

## So Near, So Far

### (Judges 18:6–31)

Everything in these chapters is the tale of corrupt religion. The Danites failed to get their inheritance because of unbelief. They were never allocated land elsewhere than in the areas mentioned in Joshua 19:41–46. The priest of Judges 18 is operating a corrupt and idolatrous cult. Any 'message' from the Levite that supposedly comes from God will be entirely worthless. The Danites are as corrupt in their religious ideas as Micah and the Levite! Everyone is doing what is wrong – only it is 'what is right in their own eyes'.

Once again we have here a feeble misguided religion, a corrupt imitation of true faith. Many years before Moses had sent out people to explore the land of Israel (Numbers 13:1–2). Judges 18:2 records a feeble imitation.

After a corrupt religion comes a vulnerable city (18:7–10). The Danites come to Laish. *'Then the five men departed and came to Laish...'*. The people of Laish are a classic example of a people who are vulnerable to defeat and destruction. They are (i) comfortable and complacent. The five men *'came to Laish, and saw the people who were there, how they dwelt in security, after the manner of the Sidonians, quiet and unsuspecting, lacking nothing that is in the earth, and possessing wealth, and how they were far from the Sidonians and had no dealings with anyone'* (18:7). Their people are (ii) careless in not being watchful, (iii) deluded by prosperity, (iv) isolated and confident in their own self-sufficiency. No doubt, the Book of Judges was thinking of military safety, but the Christian

100

cannot but see in the story the dangers for anyone anywhere of complacency, sleepiness, prosperity and isolation.

The spies bring back their report (18:8–10). Immediate invasion is recommended. The land is wide-open for attack; it is spacious and prosperous. Its people are almost inviting invasion!

A second trip to Laish is started, this time with hundreds of armed men. They camp in Judah (18:11–12). They intend to destroy the city and its inhabitants and take it for themselves.

On the way north the Danites pass Micah's house (18:13). The five spies who had been there earlier tell the rest of the men about the shrine with its valuable silver idols. 'We ought to exploit a place like that', they suggest. *'Now consider what you will do'* (18:14). They know what to do! They find the Levite and talk to him in a friendly manner (18:15). The five spies remove the silver idol and the contents of the shrine while the Levite is occupied talking to the six hundred men (18:16–17). When the priest sees what the five soldiers are doing he protests (18:18) but is told that he had best be quiet, stop complaining and come with the Danites for promotion to higher pay and a more prestigious job. The Levite is delighted with the idea, helps in the theft of the idols and joins the Danites (18:19–20). They all depart together (18:21).

At this point we might pause and reflect on the story. What is the use of a god who gets kidnapped and is carried around from one owner to another? And what is the use of a religion that allows and encourages theft, idolatry and irresponsibility? What is the use of a priest who becomes a religious professional simply for the money and the security, and who will abandon one job for another at the suggestion of better pay and advancement? But, we remind ourselves, all of this was considered 'right' in the eyes of those concerned. They did not consider they were doing anything wrong!

The fact is: religion is one of the most blinding, depraving, forces in the story of humankind. Christians need to repudiate 'religion' altogether. The Christian faith is not a matter of superstition and immoral gods. Christian faith is a matter of God's revealing Himself to us, and the first thing He reveals is that He is a holy God. Man's religiosity without guidance from God is a corrupt rotten business. This kind of 'religion' invents gods for its own purposes. It is selfish and self-centred. It has amazing power to bring blindness and deception. Can these people of Judges 18 not see what they are doing? No they cannot.

After the Danites had gone some distance, Micah called together some of his neighbours and he and his friends caught up with the Danites (18:22). But the Danites were not bothered. They coolly said 'What's your problem?' (see 18:23) and Micah – the thief of 17:1–2 – furiously complains at their theft of his home-made gods (18:24). 'You'd better quit complaining or you will get hurt', was their reply (18:25). Micah had no choice but to swallow his pride and abandon hope of seeing his god or his priest again (18:26).

The Danites continued on their way. Laish was destroyed (18:27). The vulnerability of the town now reveals itself (18:28). The Danites destroyed the city, then rebuilt it and named it after themselves (18:28b–29). Their idolatry continued. Micah's god and Micah's one-time priest and his descendants continued to keep the idolatrous cult going. It survived until 'the captivity of the land' – probably a reference to an otherwise unknown invasion, perhaps by Philistines. It continued to function despite the fact that God had a shrine at Shiloh (18:31).

Why are we told all of this?

1. It highlights the utter blindness and uselessness of religion that is 'natural' rather than revealed. Men and women are 'naturally' religious but such religion is of no value whatsoever.

2. It demonstrates how true faith gets corrupted by tradition. It was 'traditional' for Israelites to have priests. But in Micah's day their formal religion had lost touch with the Scriptural demands of the law of Moses.

3. It highlights the sin that may be found in religious people. Both the Danites and Micah were religious people. Micah was never troubled about stealing 1100 pieces of silver from his mother but is furious when something of lesser value is taken from him. The Danites want to worship the **same** gods; they are Micah's 'fellow-believers' in the same

idolatrous adulation of the same silver god. But there is no fellowship of any kind between these men in their identical veneration of the same god. The Danites rob Micah; and Micah hates them. But they are concerned to worship the same idols!

Poor Micah! He lost his god, his priest, his riches, his reputation among his neighbours – all in one day.

Yet while all of this was going on, there was a house of God at Shiloh! The tabernacle was there. It spoke of the holy glory of God which no person could approach without the blood of atonement. Deep within the tent was the law of God which spoke of His demands upon His people. The Danites, Micah and his disloyal priest were all ignorant of the true God of Israel. This is the way it is. People reject the God of the Bible but then their replacement does them no good. It would be better for them to turn to the God who reveals Himself in His tabernacle as the Holy God – the God who saved Israel by the blood of a lamb. God was so near to them – in the tabernacle. Shiloh was not far away. But they were so far from knowing Him, because they followed their own religious ideas.

# Chapter 28

# A Levite and His Concubine
(Judges 19:1–30)

We are introduced to what is perhaps the ugliest story to be found anywhere in the Bible. Judges 17–18 was bad enough. Judges 19 is worse!

The opening line of Judges 19 reminds us of the basic problem of Israel. They were without a king (19:1a). Amongst other things some kind of king could impose order. Yet Israel had neither an earthly king who would impose the will of God, nor did they have much respect for God Himself.

A Levite who lived in Ephraim took a Judahite concubine (19:1). She was a loose-living girl who 'played the harlot against him' (as the Hebrew says) and eventually went back home to Judah (19:2). Four months later the Levite travelled to Judah seeking to get her back (19:3–4). Israelite hospitality was such that the Judean father-in-law persuaded the son-in-law to stay for a fourth and a fifth night (19:5–9), but on the fifth night the man insisted on leaving (19:10). They were travelling late at night, came near to Jerusalem (at that time occupied by non-Israelites) but thought they should not stay in an alien town and so went on to Gibeah, an Israelite town (19:11–14). There they were given no hospitality and were planning to stay the night in the open square in the centre of town (19:15). An old man – not a Benjamite but an Ephraim-ite – discovered them there and asked how they came to be there (19:16–17). The Levite explained. He was on his way home with his wife (19:18–19). He did not need provisions but he did need some shelter. He was on his way home.[1] Since the

elder man was from Ephraim himself he was happy to give the
younger man hospitality (19:20–21).

Then a ghastly story follows. The men of the city were
disgustingly obscene men and wanted to homosexually abuse
the visiting stranger (19:22). So appallingly sordid was the
culture of the day, two girls were offered instead (19:23–24).
The townsmen refused but the Levite pushed the girl out and
the townsmen abused her violently and then left her to the
cold of the night. Soon she died (19:25–28a). The Levite from
Ephraim went home with the body (19:28b), dismembered the
corpse and sent pieces to twelve districts of the land, presumably the areas of the twelve tribes (19:29). There must have
gone out too some kind of explanation as to why the woman's
body was being treated in this way. The chapter concludes by
telling us of how shocked the nation was. The general opinion
was: it was the worst event that had ever taken place since the
beginning of the nation (19:30).

1. **It is a picture of total ethical collapse**. Some time ago
Israel had been redeemed by the blood of the lamb and given
a law by God which, although it was not perfect, should have
maintained morality in the land. But now the situation is one
of total moral collapse. The nation is without anyone to
impose law (19:1a). A Levite who is never meant to marry an
immoral girl is taking an unstable loose-living girl as a
concubine. Hospitality in Gibeah is nil, and the city of Gibeah
turns out to be more dangerous than the Jebusite town which
the travellers feared (19:11–14). The men of Gibeah are
homosexual, violent, uncompassionate and murderous. The
Levite treats his slave-wife as a nonentity whom he virtually
owns. Although she is said to be immoral he does not handle
her immorality in accordance with the Mosaic law (see
Deuteronomy 22:21). He wants her back as a sexual partner
and a housekeeper and yet ignores her and treats her
despicably. The woman's father takes no action to deal with
her immorality. The two men of the story disregard the slave-
concubine while they are enjoying their festivities. The woman
is immoral and disloyal to her husband, but the men of
the story have no concern for the women whatsoever and the
story is hideously cruel to the women involved. The treatment

of the woman by the townsmen was punishable by death according to the Mosaic law. Although the nation was shocked and thought it was the worst event that had ever taken place since the beginning of the nation (19:30), yet the truth was that that was what they had come to. That is what they really were! The story reminds us – and is intended to do so – of the story of Sodom in Genesis 19. A town in northern Israel has become an Israelite Sodom!

2. **Lack of kingship is the reason given for collapse of righteousness**. Several times the book of Judges has pointed to the absence of a king. The reason why everyone was doing what was right in his own eyes was because there was no king to uphold righteousness.

3. **The Levite and his wife were without help or hope**. There were no angels to deliver the Levite and his concubine that night, as there had been for Lot in a similar situation. Abraham had been praying for Lot, and Lot was (more or less) a righteous man. But there is no intercessor watching over the Levite and his wife, and there is nothing specially righteous about their lifestyle. A town in Israel has become a Sodom, but the people in trouble and distress are not in a position to look to God for deliverance.

We are getting near the end of Judges. What a long way we are – spiritually as well as in the number of pages! – from Abraham and Joseph and Moses and Joshua. What dark ugly stories can be told of this time in Israel's history. A nation that has no king, no Saviour, no guide, no rescuer in times of trouble – what depths of desperate need they can fall into. There are parts of our world that are not so different.

## Note

[1] The Hebrew has 'to the house of Yahweh'. The Greek has 'to my home'. This suggests that at some stage *bty* ('my house') was mistakenly read as an abbreviation for *bt Yhwh* ('house of Yahweh').

# Chapter 29

## Reaping Destruction

(Judges 20:1–21:25)

The sin of Gibeah leads to civil war. The entire nation responds to the disgusting and murderous ways of Gibeah. The appeal of the Levite that the nation should take action against Gibeah receives a response. The entire nation responds to the summons of the Levite and gather at Mizpah (20:1). A large number of representatives come, probably 'four hundred officers' (the Hebrew word for 'thousand' can sometimes mean 'officer' and that meaning fits here). The Levite tells his story (20:4–7), presenting himself in a good light (compare 20:5 with 19:25). The assembly resolves to punish Gibeah (20:8–11); the people of Gibeah show no remorse (20:12–13). The people of Benjamin gather to fight (20:14–16); the rest of Israel does the same (20:17).

They consult the LORD, using the Urim and Thummim, and Judah is chosen to be the leader in the battle (20:18). It reminds us of Judges 1:1–2, only at that stage of events God guidance was a means of blessing. At this stage God is giving them what they want and guiding them into His judgement!

The Benjamites are skilful warriors and Israel suffers many losses. They grieve over the fact that they are fighting their brothers but the LORD confirms this is what they must do (20:19–23). A second attack was unsuccessful (20:24–25). Only at a third attempt do they succeed in defeating Benjamin (20:26–48).[1] The tribe of Benjamin was almost annihilated.

107

The story seems to have been given as a sample of the judgement of God. Several times in the Book of Judges we have been told that God got angry with Israel or that He let them fall into the hands of their enemies. This story seems to be told as another sample of God's anger.

**When God is angry with His people they lose their wisdom**. It was true that the callous brutality of the people of Benjamin required some kind of punishment, but the nation almost wiped out the whole tribe! The LORD gave victory against the Benjamites only on the third attempt. The remainder of the nation was being punished as well as Benjamin. We have read in Judges of times when Israel's enemies virtually destroyed each other (see 7:22). Something similar is happening here. When God is angry the nation starts destroying itself.

**When God is angry with His people they become full of contradictions**. First they want to destroy Benjamin; then they are troubled at the near extermination of the tribe. The Benjamites were almost wiped out. What had been done shattered the unity of the nation. They had taken needlessly extreme measures. Yet they felt they had to keep their vows. At Mizpah they had sworn not to give any daughter in marriage to any Benjamite (21:1). They call a meeting at Bethel, where they express their grief at what has happened (21:2–3). Then they dedicate themselves to God with whole burnt offerings (symbolising dedication) and fellowship offerings (symbolising fellowship together, 21:4). The meeting is taken very seriously; the death penalty will fall on anyone who does not attend (21:5).

The gathering was grieving over the lost tribe (21:6) and wondering how to provide wives for the survivors (21:7). Apparently there were surviving men but no surviving women. Then they discovered that the men of Jabesh Gilead have not come to the meeting (21:8–9). They send fighting men to wipe out that community also! It is strange that having wiped out Benjamin they now feel they should wipe out Jabesh Gilead also! But if they do so there will be some unmarried ladies who survive and this will solve their problem about brides for the surviving Benjamites. Four hundred

young ladies survived this slaughter and they helped provide
wives for the Benjamites (21:10–14). It is all weird procedure.
They had punished Benjamin because of the sexual abuse of
the Levite's concubine, but now are happy for four hundred
women to be drastically taken from one tribe to another and
handed over to strangers as wives. Their entire behaviour is
full of blindness and contradictions.

But there were still not enough wives for the Benjamite
men, so their next remedy was to make use of a countryside
festival near Shiloh (21:15–19). The Benjamites were allowed
to hide in the bushes and at the appropriate time seize wives
from among the young dancing girls who come to assist at the
celebrations (21:20). The plan is that when the girls' brothers
and fathers complain, it will be explained that this was a way
of securing the future of the tribe of Benjamin without
breaking a vow (21:21–22)! Apparently this explanation will
be satisfactory! So that is what happened and the matter was
settled (21:23–24). The narrator brings the book to a close by
recalling what he said at the start of this unit: there was no
king (21:25; see 19:1); everyone did what was right in his own
eyes. By this time we are seeing what he means!

**When God is angry with His people they need a King to save
them**. The Book of Judges tells the story of how Israel
declined between Joshua and Samuel. If it had not been
written we would not know how Israel had got from doing
so well (Joshua and the battle of Jericho) to doing so badly
(Eli and the totally corrupt state of Israel). By the time we
reach Judges 21, we have certainly got the writer's point. A
nation without unity and without kingship had slipped into
the most vile and ghastly depravity. Those who sow to the
flesh shall from the flesh reap ruination (see Galatians 6:8).
The last pages of Judges let us see what such 'destruction'
might involve: loss of numbers, painful experiences of many
kinds, wandering in the half-light of having only partial
guidance from God, gross ignorance of God and His ways.

By now we ought to be convinced: what Israel needs is
kingship! They need a righteous Shepherd-King to bring
them back into the ways of God. The next book of the Bible,
1–2 Samuel, will show how God got to a man of His own

heart, a shepherd who would unite Israel and bring it back into the ways of the LORD. But even David will not be a complete answer, for his descendants will ruin what he did. It all points to the need of a different kind of king, a Son of David who would bring in, not partial and temporary righteousness, but eternal righteousness. The worst story in the Bible points us to Jesus. The worst sins need the best Saviour. He comes to call, not the righteous, but the kind of people we find in Judges 20–21.

## Note

[1] 'Phineas' in Judges 20:28 might make us think this story took place early in the days of Judges. But the Phineas of Numbers 25 surely would not have been passive in a situation like this. And Judges gives the impression that the chaos of chapters 20–21 is the outcome of great deterioration not its beginning. More likely it is a different Phineas in the same line, named after the more famous one of Numbers 25. 'Son' means 'descendant'. We note that Eli also named one of his sons 'Phineas' (1 Samuel 1:2).

# Chapter 30

## A Woman Who Needed a Redeemer
### (Ruth 1:1–22)

The Book of Ruth tells the story of a woman, whose husband and sons died after they had all emigrated to Moab. Ruth her daughter-in-law was intensely loyal to her and adopted Naomi's country and faith as her own (Ruth 1:1–18). The two women left Moab and went to Bethlehem in Judah, arriving at the time of the barley harvest (1:19–22). As a poor woman, Ruth was allowed to collect the scraps from the harvest. In the course of doing so she was noticed by Boaz who owned the fields (2:1–7). He was kind to her, knowing of her devotion to her mother-in-law (2:8–16). Naomi knew him as a kinsman and urged Ruth to remain close to his workers during the harvest time (2:17–23). At Naomi's suggestion, Ruth asked Boaz to be her redeemer-husband. He was willing but told her that there was a nearer kinsman who had to be consulted (3:1–18). Boaz settled the matter with the nearer kinsman and publicly took Ruth as his wife (4:1–12). Ruth soon gave birth to a son, an heir for Naomi (4:13–17a) and (as it turned out) the grandfather of king David (4:17b). The book closes with the genealogy of David, traced through Obed the son of Boaz and Ruth (4:18–22).

There must have been many family-stories like this one, passed down from father to son. The first people who told the story could never have dreamed that millions of people would be reading it thousands of years later, in hundreds of different languages.

How did it come to have a place in our Bibles? The story must have been written down in the days of David (as 4:17–22 shows) but before the days of Solomon (who would also have been mentioned if the book were that late). It would have been valued because of its connection with David. It explained how he came to be descended from a Moabitess.

Yet in the providence of God it has other purposes. It shows how God has purposes of incorporating gentiles into His people, and did so even in the family of David himself.

It show us too how redemption works. A redeemer has to have at least three qualifications. (i) He must have the **power** to redeem. (ii) He must have the legal **right** to redeem. And (iii) he must have the **desire** to redeem. Boaz illustrates the three points perfectly. No wonder the Christian sees Jesus on every page of the Book of Ruth. It constantly reminds him of One who had the power to redeem, who stepped into our humanity and became a Kinsman-Redeemer, and who redeems us because He wants to redeem us. One can see how it would come to be attached to Judges. After the terrible stories of Judges 17–21, the Book of Ruth when added to Judges gives Judges-Ruth a happy ending!

So as we open the pages of the Book of Ruth, we meet a woman who needed a redeemer.

1. **God has mysterious purposes even in the greatest of troubles**. As we read the early pages of the book, we are struck by the way in which everyone is suffering and facing adversity. It is set in the days of chaos, when the judges ruled (1:1). Added to the chaotic ways of the nation is a time of famine, which brought greater distress (1:1). Elimelech took his family elsewhere to escape the famine (1:2), but the emigration did not work out well. Elimelech died (1:3). Their two sons died (1:4). Nothing seemed to work well for Naomi.

Was there anything wrong in their going to Moab? Well, it is hard to see anything sinful in trying to get food when a country is in famine. And yet nothing that the family did brought them the relief they sought. Marrying Moabite girls was definitely not a good idea; they would have no faith in the

God of Israel. Orphah certainly worshipped the gods of Moab (see 1:15). It seems that the family ruined their life – and three of them lost their lives – in their attempt to make things easier for themselves.

And yet the rest of the story will make it clear that God has purposes in the greatest of tragedies. He is even able to make our mistakes turn around for good. I doubt whether Elimelech did the right thing in going to Moab, and yet as a result of all that happened, God's king, David turned out to be part-gentile in ancestry. His great-grandmother was a Moabitess. God loves to overrule in distressing situations, and 'work all things together for good' according to His purpose to bring a Saviour to the world.

2. **So we see how God slowly began to work**. The time came when the end of all of Naomi's troubles was near at hand. The famine ended! Naomi got to hear about it (1:6). Somehow it is possible for her to go back. Troublesome days may last a long time, but when God decides to bring them to an end, events begin to move fast!

Some good came out of what happened. Ruth came to faith in the God of Israel. A Moabitess was converted to faith in Yahweh, and insistently told Naomi 'Your God will be my God'. God can bring wonderful things even out of tragedies.

Naomi started to go home. Her daughters-in-law came part way (1:7) but Naomi wanted to release them and let them stay in Moab (1:8). There was no point in their coming with her (1:9–13). Orphah sees the sense in what Naomi says and leaves (1:14). But Ruth has come to faith in Yahweh. She is determined to have Yahweh as her God, Israel as her home, Naomi as her closest friend (1:15–18).

They arrive in Bethlehem (1:19–22). Naomi confesses (if we may understand verse 21 in this way) that their going to Moab was a mistake. She was 'full' at the time of their going, but the family panicked and left Israel prematurely. But we can already feel that God is at work, and that things are going to work out well. The family left in a famine, and disaster followed. Now a smaller family arrives at harvest time (1:22), and we can feel that God is about to reverse everything that had happened. He can step in, in the midst of tragedies and work wonders, for those who are in His purpose. He is able to work all things together for good.

# Chapter 31

## Finding a Redeemer

(Ruth 2:1–23)

When God begins to work He makes up for lost time. Things move fairly speedily once Ruth comes to the land of Israel.

1. **A redeemer is at hand for Ruth but she is unaware of his graciousness**. Boaz is nearby (2:1); the reader is told of him. But Ruth herself knows nothing of him at this stage.

However Ruth knows that she is permitted to 'glean' (that is, 'pick up the scraps') after the harvesters have done their work of reaping in the barley fields.

Naomi had a 'kinsman', a relative by marriage. He had the ability and wealth to 'redeem' her, to take her as wife, to relieve her anxieties as a poor woman, to be a husband and protector for her. Because she had come to faith in Yahweh, and had joined the people of God as a believer in the God of Israel, there was provision for her protection. She was entitled to care and safekeeping within the people of Israel. Boaz was nearby and he was 'a mighty man of substance' (2:1).

She was looking for grace. *'Let me go ... following the one in whose sight I may find grace ... '* (2:2). She was looking for favour from the owner of the land. But she did not know much about Boaz at this point. Boaz was an earthly redeemer. The God of Israel is a Redeemer. 'Their Redeemer is strong; Yahweh the Almighty is his name' (Jeremiah 50:34). The kinsmen-redeemers of the Israelite legal system was simply a way in which Israel's divine Redeemer provided for the needy among His people.

2. **Ruth finds the graciousness she is looking for in a kinsman-redeemer**. She starts 'gleaning' in a nearby field of barley.

**She 'happens' to meet Boaz**. Verse 3 says *'Her chance was to come to part of a field belonging to Boaz . . . '*. The Book of Ruth is drawing our attention to the hidden providence of God. Ruth herself was not manipulating or arranging anything for herself. She came to Boaz's field by 'chance' (that is, it was an unintentional happening on her part; of course it was not 'chance' to God').

**She discovers his concern**. Boaz is a gracious man, friendly to his workers (2:4). He notices the girl (2:5) and the workers tell him who she is (2:6). Verse 7 (which is difficult in Hebrew) could be taken as follows. *'She said* [earlier in the day] *"Please let me glean and gather after the reapers among the sheaves." She came and has kept waiting from morning till now. She has not been at home at all today!'* This makes sense of the Hebrew without amending the text. It means that Ruth has asked permission to do some **extra** gleaning for the sake of Naomi. Ruth has some of the energy and initiative which will reappear in her great-grandson!

Boaz responds warmly. Ruth is welcomed and urged to make good use of Boaz's field (2:8). He is concerned about her safety, and that she should not get too thirsty (2:9). She is amazed at his kindliness to a foreigner who has only just arrived in Judah (2:10).

**She discovers his knowledge**. Boaz in fact knows all about her. He knows about her sufferings; he knows she has come to faith in the God of Israel (2:11). He knows she is seeking refuge under the wings of the God of Israel (2:12). His kindness and his knowledge take all of her fears and anxieties away (2:13).

**She discovers his continuing practical compassion towards her**. He takes further steps to see that she is provided for. His servants will keep her company (2:14a). He himself will attend to the needs of this newly arrived Moabitess (2:14b). He ensures that no one will ill-treat her (2:15) and makes sure that she has some extra provision (2:16). At the end of the day she has done well because of Boaz's generosity (2:17).

3. **She has found that her kinsman-redeemer rewards the humble**. What led to Ruth's experiencing so much of the graciousness of Boaz. Initially it was her faith in the God of Israel. If she had never said to Naomi 'Your God will be my God', these things could not even have started to happen!

But it was not only Ruth's faith; it was Ruth's 'good works' as well. He faith in being 'under the wings of Yahweh' have led her into ways of humility. She is content to be a gleaner. She humbly trusts in the graciousness of Boaz. She admits her need.

Ruth is generous towards Naomi, in sharing what she has gleaned (2:18). Naomi on her part gives her some encouraging information. She tells Ruth that the one she has met is in fact a 'kinsman', someone who is entitled, and perhaps even obliged, to take on Ruth as a husband and a redeemer (2:19–20). Boaz's advice has been good. 'Stay close to my servants' he had said (2:21). Ruth took Naomi's advice and kept away from anywhere where she might face abuse or insult (2:22). In this way she continued throughout the barley harvest and through to the end of the wheat harvest (2:23).

The story has been a sweet tale of a woman finding a kinsman-redeemer. Her faith brought her within reach of his graciousness. Her humility attracted his attention. The redeemer and the widow are both behaving in a way that is likely to bring them together.

In all of this the Christian learns lessons about loyalty and kindness, diligence and compassion. The three characters, Naomi, Boaz and Ruth, are all attractive people.

But there is more than good example in all of this. God's word is giving us a portrayal of what it means for someone to be a redeemer. Every aspect of Boaz is wonderful in itself, and reminds us of Jesus before Jesus came to this world. Faithful believers get to be like Jesus – even before Jesus was born.

Our Redeemer, Jesus, is at hand. His graciousness is greater than we ever realised. He too is full of concern, and knows all about us. He too will continue in faithfulness and compassion towards us. Faith opens up the way for all of the blessings of

His redemption. Humble dependence – and even staying close to His servants – will bring to us an abundant 'reaping' from His fields, which we may share with others. We too hide under the wings of Yahweh.

# Chapter 32

## Asking for Redemption
### (Ruth 3:1–18)

At this stage in the story Ruth has now become aware of this
'kinsman-redeemer' who is so gracious towards her. At first
she was hardly aware that 'redemption' was involved in her
coming to faith in the God of Israel. Then she became aware
of his knowledge and concern about her. Now the story takes
a step forward.

1. **Ruth enquires after the blessings of redemption**. Naomi is
very conscious that Ruth needs a 'redeemer'. She approaches
Ruth with a suggestion. Ruth must ask Boaz to 'redeem' her,
to take her as his wife. Naomi knows the benefits of being
'redeemed' by Boaz.

**Ruth needs 'rest'**. The initiative is taken by Naomi. *'My
daughter, should I not seek "rest" for you, so that it may be well
with you...?'* (3:1). Ruth needs to be able to have an
assurance of provision, an assurance of protection. One of
the blessings of redemption is 'entering into rest'. When
blessing is guaranteed the beneficiary 'enters into rest'. There
is such an assurance of blessing that the person receiving the
benefits 'rests' – enters into total confidence that good things
are at hand.

**The 'rest' will come when a kinsman-redeemer takes his
responsibility and does the work of redeeming**. Naomi now
wants Boaz to fully play a part in Ruth's life as kinsman-
redeemer. 'Is not Boaz our kinsman?' says Naomi. There is
hope that Boaz will specially take responsibility for Ruth
because he is related to the family and **part of the work of**

**being a kinsman-redeemer is to marry the childless widow**.
Naomi tells Ruth she must prepare herself as a desirable
young woman. She must put on some perfume and some nice
clothes, and go to the 'threshing floor' where Boaz is staying
overnight, since there is much work to be done there at
harvest time (3:3). She must go down there but keep away
from where Boaz is sleeping until very late at night. She must
wait until Boaz has had supper and is feeling relaxed and
ready for his night's sleep. Then Ruth is to go and uncover his
feet and lie down at the lower end of his bed (3:4). It is a piece
of symbolism. It is a way of saying, 'Would you not like to
have me as your wife and as the one who shares your bed?'
Naomi tells Ruth to make this symbolic proposal and then
leave the rest to Boaz.

Why did Ruth have to do things this way? Why could Boaz
not be approached in a more straightforward manner? It
probably has to do with the fact that Ruth was a foreigner.
Boaz had obviously greatly admired Ruth (as Ruth 2 makes
clear) but did not know how to respond to this Moabitess.
Naomi's plan was to get Ruth to be highly attractive, and then
do something that challenged Boaz to act speedily.

Ruth does as Naomi asks (3:5–6). She lies down at the
lower part of his bed (3:7). He wakes up and finds Ruth lying
at his feet (3:8), She asks him to marry her because he is a
kinsman-redeemer (3:9). It is put clearly in verse 9. Part of the
work of a redeemer is to marry the widowed, childless relative.

The story is suspenseful in its own right, but it also throws
light on the Christian's redemption. The Christian's relationship to Jesus is like the marriage relationship. The Christian is
'married' to Jesus (see Romans 7:4). Without such a relationship to Jesus the Christian will be fruitless; he or she will
produce no 'offspring' for God. But by being released from
the Mosaic law (Romans 7:1–4), and by being joined to Jesus,
he or she bears fruit for God.

**The reason why Ruth expects to be 'redeemed' in this way is
that Boaz is a kinsman**. Family relationship leads to responsibility as a redeemer. Jesus' incarnation was necessary for Him
to be our redeemer. Jesus has to become one with us if He is to
be our redeemer.

2. **Next we see Boaz' response**. He thanks her! He is delighted with the idea of taking her as his wife and 'redeeming' her. He is so grateful she has not sought protection from anyone else (3:10). She wants to be redeemed by one who is truly qualified to be her redeemer. She is not seeking redemption anywhere else. No younger man has enticed her (3:11).

Though he is delighted at the thought of being her 'redeemer', he has to do it in a legal manner. There is someone who has a higher claim to be kinsman than he has (3:12). Ruth may stay close to him for that night. Soon he will see to it that redemption will be provided for Ruth (3:13). She gets some rest (3:14a) but leaves early so that Boaz will not be embarrassed by difficult questions (3:14b). He abundantly provides for her (3:15). She goes and tells the story to Naomi (3:16–17) who is confident that Boaz will speedily do what is right.

Some important aspects of redemption surface at this point. Redemption is based on relationship. Redemption has to be legal. These two points are vital to the Christian's redemption which operates at a much deeper level. Jesus could not have redeemed us without becoming one with us. He had to be our kinsman before He could be our redeemer.

The story is based on the custom of 'Levirate marriage' (or something very similar to it). In ancient Israel a childless widow might marry her dead husband's brother. It would enable her to bear children and not be childless. It gave her security. It is a custom which still continues in parts of the world.

The story helps us to understand our own salvation. Jesus is delighted to be our redeemer. He came into this world as our kinsman in order that He might do the work of rescuing us from our plight. We may apply to Him to do the work of redeeming us when we are in distress in this wicked world.

# Chapter 33

## Redemption Accomplished
### (Ruth 4:1–22)

Boaz now has to deal with obstacles to his redeeming Ruth. One gets a strong impression from Ruth chapter 2 that Boaz had the greatest admiration for Ruth. Ruth herself has proposed to him that he should be her kinsman-redeemer, and therefore her husband. There is no hint of any other wife of Boaz; yet he is obviously older than Ruth. Everything is set for a happy union – except that there is one obstacle. A kinsman-redeemer has to do things in a legal manner and there is someone who is more entitled to redeem Ruth than Boaz is.

There is obviously some connection between the marriage of Boaz and Ruth and the custom of 'Levirate' marriage ('brother-in-law' marriage) mentioned in Deuteronomy 25. The two may not be 100% identical, but obviously they are very similar types of marriage.

Boaz goes to the gate of the town, the place where legal matters were settled. Very soon – God is still working speedily for Ruth – the 'next of kin' comes by. Boaz takes his chance and speaks to him (4:1). He arranges for some witnesses (4:2) and then tells the next of kin about some land that needs to be 'redeemed' (4:3). When land was leased to someone outside of the family, it was the duty of the 'next of kin' to do what he could to 'redeem' it – buy it back so as to keep it in the family.

'Redeemers' had at least four duties to their relatives. (i) To redeem a close family member who had fallen into slavery;

122

(ii) to redeem a close family member from landlessness; (iii) to redeem a close family member from childlessness if her husband died prematurely, (iv) to redeem a close family member from loss of life, if his life could be rescued by the payment of a price (see Exodus 13:13b).

One can see how God could be called Israel's 'Redeemer'. He too rescues His people from the death sentence (for the wages of sin is death), from landlessness (for our salvation involves a 'new heavens and new earth', and even now 'all things are ours'). He rescues us from barrenness (we are 'joined to another so as to bear fruit for God'). In many ways God in Christ is our 'kinsman-redeemer'. In elucidating 'redemption', the Book of Ruth enables us to see Jesus with new eyes.

Boaz has two of these responsibilities on his mind, but he has good reasons for mentioning the land first.

Naomi is extremely poor. She could improve her position by selling some land, but it would be best if her closest relative were to become her 'kinsman-redeemer' and buy the land so as to keep it within the family. It is this proposal that Boaz puts to the 'next of kin' (4:4). The next-of-kin is happy to acquire some land in this way. But then Boaz says to him *'On the day that you acquire the field from the hand of Naomi and from Ruth the Moabitess, you acquire the widow of the deceased husband in order to continue the name of the man who has died in connection with his property* (4:5).

At this the next-of-kin is alarmed. He does not want to bring into the world a rival to his own son. He withdraws his interest in Naomi's land and urges Boaz to buy it – plus Ruth (4:6)! The removal of the sandal was his final and legal renunciation of any claim to the land – or to Ruth (4:7–8). Boaz makes sure that all of his witnesses have clearly understood what has happened. He has 'bought all the property'. And he has 'acquired Ruth' (4:9–10). The witnesses confirm what has been legally settled (4:11a) and they pray for Yahweh's blessing on the marriage (4:11b–12).

A gracious redeemer will remove all obstacles to his redemption going forward. Boaz wishes to redeem Ruth. He overcomes obstacles and difficulties in the way.

Soon the couple were married; a son was born (4:13). It was regarded as being a son for Naomi (4:14). Ruth's love for Naomi is obvious to everyone (4:15), and the new-born grandchild is given to Naomi (4:16–17). The suffering with which our book began (Ruth 1:1–5) has been eradicated and overruled for good.

Ruth 4:18 traces the family line from Perez to David, running through Boaz and Obed, Ruth's son. David was Ruth's great-grandson. David had some Moabite blood in his veins.

The famine which led to Elimelech's leaving Israel, and which brought so much trouble and distress into his family, had an unusual purpose in it. It was God's way of allowing a gentile into His kingdom, and even into the family line of His Son. The story began with famine and death; it ends with restoration, abundance and newness of life. Secretly and inconspicuously God had been working all the time. In the lives of these quite ordinary people God had a purpose to bring David to Israel. In Judges we are reminded that there was no king in Israel, and as a result chaos prevailed. In the Book of Ruth, the story begins by mentioning the chaotic day 'when the judges ruled' (1:1). This brings to our mind all sorts of calamities and chaos. But the story ends by reminding us that Boaz and Ruth's marriage will soon lead to David, a king in the land, the very thing Israel needs. Despite the faithlessness of the days when the judged rules, God has been faithful to them. He raises up a half-Israelite, half-gentile couple, Boaz and Ruth. Into that line He will send his Son, His Saviour. Ruth a gentile who sought refuge under the wings of Yahweh was given a kinsman-redeemer to meet all her needs. Her story provides illumination for the Christian who is redeemed from death, distress and disaster by a kinsman who drives away any claims from any rival; who might take us to himself. Then our heavenly Boaz buys us for Himself, and we bear fruit unto God.

# Some Further Reading

Commentaries for preachers on Judges include Herbert Wolf's work in the *Expositor's Bible Commentary*, vol. 3 (Zondervan, 1992) and C.J. Goslinga's *Joshua, Judges, Ruth* (Zondervan, 1986). D.R. Davis, *Such a Great Salvation* (Baker, 1990) is more significant than its chatty style suggests; it is a good book for preachers. B.F.C. Atkinson's *Judges and Ruth* (1969) has always been one of my favourite commentaries; it is delightfully eccentric at times but is always interesting and profitable. Some will despise it, but I love it. A. Cundall and L. Morris wrote *Judges, Ruth* for the Tyndale Commentaries series (Tyndale, 1968). G.J. Keddie's *Even in Darkness: Judges and Ruth...* (Evangelical Press, 1985) is simple but may be recommended.

L.R. Klein, *The Triumph of Irony in the Book of Judges* (Almond, 1988) is thought-provoking. B.J. Webb's work in the *New Bible Commentary – 21st Century Edition* builds on Webb's *The Book of Judges: an Integrated Reading* (JSOT, 1987). C.F. Keil's *Joshua, Judges and Ruth* is very dated, but it is still more helpful than many modern equivalents.

Commentaries by J.A. Soggin, G.F. Moore, R.G. Boling, J. Gray, A.G. Auld, are useful in some ways but may be left aside by most preachers. C.F. Burney's *Book of Judges* (1918) is still interesting but may also be left aside.

More expository material is best found in M. Wilcock, *The Message of Judges* (IVP, 1992) and in Matthew Henry's famous commentary.

In a class all of its own is the old Puritan work by Rogers. It is a difficult work to read and needs immense patience and zeal to work through it. I found it more difficult than many Puritan works I have read; but for those who have the patience it can be recommended.

The two best technical commentaries on Ruth are easily the works by Hubbard (published by Eerdmans) and Campbell (Anchor Bible, Doubleday). M.D. Gow's *The Book of Ruth* (IVP, 1992) is also worth consulting.